ABC OF ALCOHOL

Fourth Edition

Edited by

ALEX PATON

Retired consultant physician, Oxfordshire

ROBIN TOUQUET

Consultant in accident and emergency medicine, St Mary's Hospital, London

BMJ
Books

Blackwell
Publishing

© 1982, 1988, 1994 BMJ Publishing Group
© 2005 by Blackwell Publishing Ltd
BMJ Books is an imprint of the BMJ Publishing Group Limited, used under licence

Blackwell Publishing, Inc., 350 Main Street, Malden, Massachusetts 02148-5020, USA
Blackwell Publishing Ltd, 9600 Garsington Road, Oxford OX4 2DQ, UK
Blackwell Publishing Asia Pty Ltd, 550 Swanston Street, Carlton, Victoria 3053, Australia

First published 1982
Second edition 1988
Third edition 1994
Fourth edition 2005
2   2007

Library of Congress Cataloging-in-Publication Data

ABC of alcohol/edited by Alex Paton, Robin Touquet.—4th ed.
     p. ; cm.
   Includes bibliographical references and index.
   ISBN: 978-0-7279-1814-7 (alk. paper)

1. Alcoholism. 2. Alcohol—Physiological effect.
   [DNLM: 1. Alcoholism—diagnosis—Great Britain. 2. Alcoholism—therapy—Great Britain. 3. Alcohol
Drinking—adverse effects—Great Britain. 4. Alcohol Drinking—epidemiology—Great Britain.
5. Socioeconomic Factors—Great Britian. WM 274 A134 2005] I. Paton, Alex. II. Touquet, Robin.
RC565.A23 2005
616.86′1—dc22

                                                                                    2004025859

ISBN: 978 0 7279 1814 7

A catalogue record for this title is available from the British Library

Cover image is courtesy of Damien Lovegrove/Science Photo Library

Set in 9/11 pt by Newgen Imaging Systems (P) Ltd, Chennai, India
Printed and bound in India by Replika Press Pvt. Ltd

Commissioning Editor: Eleanor Lines
Development Editors: Sally Carter/Nick Morgan
Production Controller: Kate Charman

For further information on Blackwell Publishing, visit our website:
http://www.blackwellpublishing.com

Contents

Contributors　　　　　　　　　　　　　　　　　　　　　　vii

Preface　　　　　　　　　　　　　　　　　　　　　　　　ix

1　Alcohol use: consumption and costs　　　　　　　　　　1
Eric Appleby

2　Alcohol use: society and politics　　　　　　　　　　　4
Eric Appleby

3　Alcohol in the body　　　　　　　　　　　　　　　　　7
Alex Paton

4　Definitions　　　　　　　　　　　　　　　　　　　　10
Alex Paton

5　Nature of alcohol use　　　　　　　　　　　　　　　　13
Alex Paton

6　Detecting misuse　　　　　　　　　　　　　　　　　　16
Alex Paton

7　Problems in accident and emergency departments　　　　22
Robin Touquet

8　Medical problems　　　　　　　　　　　　　　　　　　26
Alex Paton

9　Surgical problems　　　　　　　　　　　　　　　　　　30
James Huntley, Robin Touquet

10　Drug-alcohol interactions　　　　　　　　　　　　　　35
John Henry

11　Management of alcohol misuse in primary care　　　　　39
Geoffrey Smerdon

12　Advice and counselling　　　　　　　　　　　　　　　43
Bruce Ritson

13　Treatments　　　　　　　　　　　　　　　　　　　　46
Bruce Ritson

14　Resources　　　　　　　　　　　　　　　　　　　　49
Bruce Ritson

Index　　　　　　　　　　　　　　　　　　　　　　　　53

Contributors

Eric Appleby
Formerly chief executive, Alcohol Concern, London

John Henry
Professor of accident and emergency medicine, Imperial College, London

James Huntley
Specialist registrar in orthopaedic surgery, Edinburgh

Alex Paton
Retired consultant physician, Oxfordshire

Bruce Ritson
Consultant psychiatrist, Edinburgh

Geoffrey Smerdon
Retired general practitioner, Cornwall

Robin Touquet
Consultant in accident and emergency medicine, St Mary's Hospital, London

Preface to the fourth edition

It is 10 years since the last edition of *ABC of Alcohol* was published, and problems from misuse of alcohol have not gone away; indeed, they are statistically more frequent than they were then. An epidemic of binge drinking, a sharp rise in drinking by women, who are particularly vulnerable to physical damage, and increasing violence associated with alcohol are current causes of concern. Given the number of calories in alcoholic drinks, it may not be too fanciful to suggest that alcohol contributes to the present epidemic of obesity. Like most of the population, we enjoy a drink, but having witnessed the many harms caused by overindulgence, we have tried to produce an introduction to alcohol and its effects that will not only inform health professionals but may be of use to involved lay people and governments wanting evidence to back up action.

When *ABC of Alcohol* was first published, the objective was to encourage doctors to regard alcohol misuse as a legitimate part of professional practice. Unfortunately, that aim has not been realised fully: in some quarters, the feeling is still that doctors should not get involved. This is largely because of lack of knowledge about how misuse of alcohol affects society and people, and thus a lack of confidence in tackling misuse. *ABC of Alcohol* is designed to remedy this and to show that sympathetic management of people with problems, especially if detected early, can be a rewarding experience.

Every medical school should cover prevention and management of alcohol misuse; teaching opportunities abound in every hospital department and in general practice. Existing chapters of *ABC of Alcohol* have been revised extensively, and important sections have been added on the impact of alcohol on accident and emergency departments and most types of surgical practice, as well as the potential dangers of alcohol's interaction with drugs—legal and illegal. Alcohol misuse is indeed every doctor's business.

Finally, we have received encouraging comments in the past about the value of *ABC of Alcohol* from health and social professionals in all disciplines. As there are now some 500 voluntary alcohol agencies in England and Wales that deal with alcohol problems, which are more often social than medical, we have tried where possible to broaden the "doctor-patient" model to encompass alcohol workers and their clients. We believe that the future success of alcohol services depends on much closer cooperation between doctors and workers in the alcohol field; the latter should be able to make their expertise available to primary care trusts and hospitals.

Special thanks are due to Sally Carter for her close involvement and constructive help and to Samuel Groom for technological support in the preparation of this new edition.

Alex Paton
Robin Touquet
2004

1 Alcohol use: consumption and costs

Eric Appleby

Although doctors are primarily concerned with the physical or psychological problems of individual drinkers, the wider social consequences of alcohol misuse at the individual and population levels are of equal importance. This is not least because the numbers of problem drinkers doctors see—and the medical and other resources available to help address the problems—are dictated largely by public concerns and government responses to these wider issues. Moreover, just as doctors need to be aware of the wider factors, workers in other social care fields, including the police or social care workers, need some basic understanding of the initial physiological effects and symptoms of excessive consumption of alcohol. Armed with expert knowledge, they will then be able to act as advocates for the best use of the resources available.

Patterns of consumption

Although the United Kingdom over the last century has never been more than a moderate consumer in terms of the total amount of alcohol drunk per capita, it is nevertheless considered to have one of the more problematic relations with alcohol, as a result of the drinking patterns and style that have developed. For the first half of the 20th century, the United Kingdom was relatively abstemious, but the decades after the second world war saw a rapid increase, with per capita consumption almost doubling. The subsequent plateau from 1979 has come to an end in recent years, as consumption has again begun to creep up—when many other western European countries, such as France and Spain, are seeing significant reductions in overall consumption. Perhaps of even greater importance is the focus on "binge drinking," which is predominately seen in those aged 16-24 years: up to 40% of men's drinking occasions involve them drinking more than twice the recommended daily maximum, with social and health consequences. The number of times that men and particularly women go drinking has increased gradually, with 30% of men and 25% of women drinking on three or more days a week.

Other variations exist within the population, with people in northern regions of England tending to binge drink more than those in the south. People from minority ethnic groups are less likely to drink, and generally drink less, than the general population, although the picture changes continuously as new generations adapt and different cultures and lifestyles merge.

Morbidity and mortality

That the effects of long term heavy drinking can be serious, and even fatal, is generally well known. Less well known is the range of medical conditions to which alcohol contributes and the relatively low levels of consumption at which the risk of harm begins to be important.

Although the relation between alcohol and health undoubtedly has complexities, some types of disease have a simple dose-response relation: the greater the amount drunk, the more harm is done. This applies to the more common causes of death, such as cirrhosis, hypertension, and haemorrhagic stroke.

The total number of deaths associated with alcohol misuse in England and Wales has been estimated at 5000-40 000 per year. The precise number notoriously has been difficult to assess because of doctors' reluctance to certify alcohol as a cause of

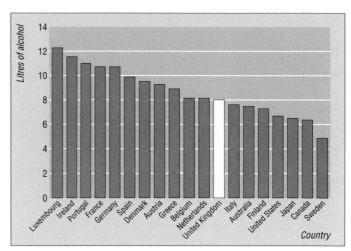

Alcohol consumption in the world in 1999: litres of pure alcohol per inhabitant

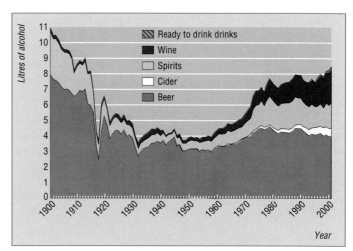

Alcohol consumption in the United Kingdom, 1900-2000: per capita consumption of pure alcohol

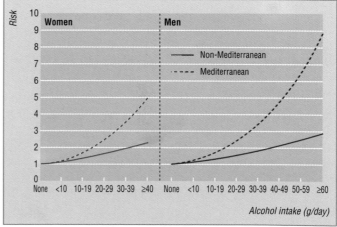

Relative risks of liver cirrhosis by level of alcohol intake

death and difficulty in defining the contribution of alcohol. The most recent calculations, carried out on behalf of the Cabinet Office Strategy Unit, place mortality at around 22 000 each year. This includes around 6000 deaths directly caused by alcohol, such as from alcoholic cirrhosis or the effects of acute intoxication, as well as attributable fractions, such as deaths in which alcohol plays a contributory role along with other factors. Included in the latter category would be cancers (for example, oesophageal and breast cancer) and some types of heart disease.

Although absolute levels of mortality may be hard to pin down, it is possible to look at trends, notably through the marker of mortality from cirrhosis. Trends in recent years suggest considerable cause for concern. Over 30 years (1970-2000), a fourfold increase was seen in deaths from cirrhosis. The biggest increase was in those aged 35-44 years, for whom the number of deaths in 2000 was 11 times that in 1970. The peak age for mortality has also shifted from those aged >55 years to those aged 45-54 years, so it would seem that changes in drinking patterns are having a significant effect, although as yet no research has been carried out to prove the link.

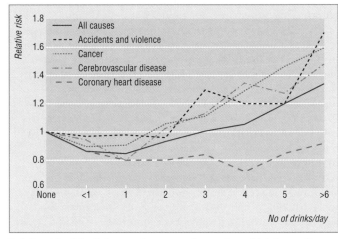

Deaths from chronic liver disease in England from 1970-2000. Changes in the coding rules for causes of death occurred in 1984 and 1993

The "protective effect"

Another side to this story exists. Alcohol, at low levels of consumption, also plays a part in protecting against certain diseases, notably coronary heart disease. Consequently, the relative risk of death is slightly lower among moderate drinkers than among total abstainers—as seen from the J shaped or U shaped curve that emerges when overall risk is set against increasing levels of consumption. Some estimates suggest that the number of deaths prevented annually as a result of the protective effect balances deaths lost through excessive drinking. This balance changes with age and, because coronary heart disease and ischaemic stroke tend to occur at later ages, most lives saved are among those aged >65 years (see Chapter 8).

The potential life years lost as a result of alcohol related deaths shows yet another picture, with up to 163 000 life years lost up to the age of 65 years and around 29 000 life years saved by the protective effect.

Relative risk of death from various causes by number of drinks per day

Burdens and costs

Internationally, the World Health Organization found that alcohol accounts for 9.2% of the overall burden of disease in developed countries. This places it third in the ranks for risk of disease: only tobacco smoking and high blood pressure pose greater risks.

Although unacceptably large numbers of people may die as a result of their use of alcohol, much greater numbers have illnesses ranging from acute toxic effects to severe mental and physical disorders. The Cabinet Office in the United Kingdom estimated that up to 150 000 hospital admissions a year are related to alcohol (see Chapters 9 and 10).

Although the association between alcohol and mental health problems is complex, links are without doubt. People who have a **pre-existing** mental health problem are more likely to drink hazardously than those without, and people who drink hazardously are more likely to **develop** a mental health problem than those who do not.

More than 30 000 hospital admissions each year are of people with alcohol dependence. These constitute just a small proportion of the estimated 2.9 million people dependent on alcohol to some degree, as defined by responses to

Some reasons for hospital admission
- Cirrhosis
- Acute and chronic pancreatitis
- Acute and chronic cardiovascular conditions
- Acute and chronic neuropsychiatric conditions
- Cancers
- Injuries received when intoxicated

In 2001, up to 1000 of 3479 deaths from suicide and self-inflicted injury were associated with misuse of alcohol

questionnaires designed to test levels of control over drinking behaviour, tolerance to the effects of alcohol impaired social functioning, and drinking to avoid withdrawal symptoms. The Royal College of Physicians identified 2-12% of all costs of NHS hospitals as attributable to alcohol.

The interaction between the health service and alcohol misuse is by no means confined to the hospital ward. Anyone familiar with emergency departments, particularly on a weekend evening, will know that doctors, nurses, and increasingly security staff spend considerable time not just treating patients but controlling the behaviour of those who are extremely intoxicated and have received an injury or been assaulted. Similarly, ambulance paramedics estimate that most of their work at these times involves dealing with the aftermath of drinking. In a recent survey, 90% themselves had experienced an assault fuelled by alcohol or seen a colleague assaulted.

In primary care, 20% of patients are likely to be excessive drinkers, and problem drinkers are known to consult general practitioners twice as often as the average patient. More disturbingly, 98% of excessive drinkers who visit surgeries are currently not identified as such. If they could be identified, strong evidence shows that brief targeted interventions could considerably reduce levels of consumption and consequent problems. The recent use of specially trained staff for screening and counselling, in general practice and hospitals, could improve the detection of drinkers at risk.

The figure showing alcohol consumption in the United Kingdom is adapted from the *BBPA Statistical Handbook*, 2001. The chart showing deaths from chronic liver disease was adapted from the *Annual report of the Chief Medical Officer* and uses data from the Office for National Statistics, department of health, 2001. The illustration showing relative risk of death from various causes by number of drinks per day is adapted from Boffetta P, Garfinkel L. *Epidemiology* 1990;1:342-8. All the other line figures in this chapter are adapted from Cabinet Office Strategy Unit. *Alcohol harm reduction project. Interim analytical report*, 2003.

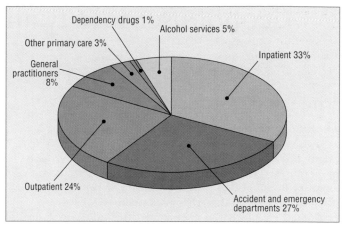

Breakdown of costs associated with misuse of alcohol

Overall cost of treating illnesses related to alcohol is £1.7 billion

2 Alcohol use: society and politics

Eric Appleby

Crime and disorder

Although the health consequences of excessive drinking are costly, the social consequences for the general public are more evident and more immediately disturbing. Alcohol misuse is linked routinely to a range of antisocial, aggressive, and violent behaviour in public and private settings. The British Crime Survey in 1999 noted that 47% of all victims of violence described their attacker as being under the influence of alcohol and calculated around 1.2 million incidents of alcohol related violence, of which 60% were not reported to the police. In many instances—over half of which took place in or around pubs—the victim and the assailant were drunk. Perhaps symptomatic of the commonness (and almost normalisation) of assaults related to alcohol is that a survey by the Home Office found that only half the people affected considered themselves to be the victims of crime and about one third saw assault related to alcohol as "just something that happens."

Assaults in the home also often are fuelled by alcohol, with a third of incidents of domestic violence taking place when the perpetrator has been drinking. Similarly, sexual assaults often take place when one or both parties have been drinking, and more than half of those convicted of rape had been drinking before they committed the crime.

Measures to tackle crime related to alcohol

The ability to predict, prevent, and tackle serious crime related to alcohol is hampered by the sheer volume of public drunkenness at peak times. The time needed to arrest and process a drunken offender not only is costly but also means that police resources on the streets are depleted while this takes place. As a result, at a time when binge drinking and other indicators of harm have increased considerably, the number of arrests for drunkenness has declined, as police seek to move large groups of unruly people out of the crowded trouble zones.

The Licensing Act 2003, which ended the regimen of "permitted hours" and enabled licensed premises to stay open until much later, was designed partially to address these problems by reducing the numbers of intoxicated people being disgorged onto the streets at a common (and, arguably, early) closing time. Many commentators are sceptical as to whether this will have any immediate effect. Instead, questions are raised about the planning decisions, often driven by a desire to regenerate rundown town centres, which lead to an accumulation of pubs and bars—all catering for a young, heavy drinking clientele—in a compact area of a town or city centre.

Despite the decline in arrests for drunkenness, more than half of probation service caseloads comprise offenders with alcohol problems. Little help has been offered to offenders inside or outside prison, despite the obvious burden that they impose at all points of the criminal justice system. Particularly noticeable has been the absence of any initiatives designed to influence the behaviour of those who persistently cause problems by becoming intensively and aggressively drunk. A two pronged initiative is under way that involves fines for drunkenness under antisocial behaviour legislation and pilot courses to modify the behaviour of persistent offenders. Courses are modelled on those successfully targeted at drink driving offenders. Although courses for drink drivers have been effective in reducing reoffending, around 500 people are still killed each year as a result of drink driving. The number of

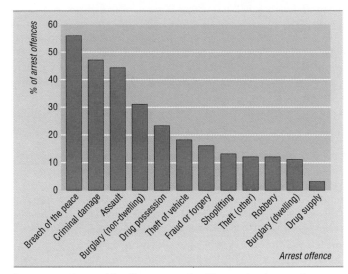

Percentage of arrestable offences committed by people who tested positive for alcohol in urine screening, 1986-2001

Despite increasing prominence being given to the practice of various drugs being used to incapacitate potential victims, alcohol remains by far the most common "date rape" drug

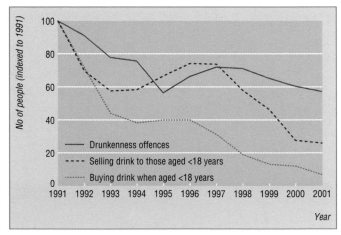

People found guilty or cautioned for offences specifically related to alcohol

Of those who end up in prison, almost two thirds of men and more than one third of women have problems with alcohol

drink drive fatalities fell consistently in the years after the introduction of the breathalyser in 1967, but this seemed to reach a plateau in the mid-1990s and the number of lesser casualties has begun to increase again. Overall, the United Kingdom has a reasonably good record in preventing drink driving compared with other European countries; the government has used this as justification for maintaining one of the highest legal blood alcohol limits in the western world. Despite strong and widely accepted evidence that the risk of an accident increases substantially at a level of alcohol in blood of 50 mg/100 ml, the government has stuck rigidly to the 80 mg limit in the belief that a reduction would be unpopular.

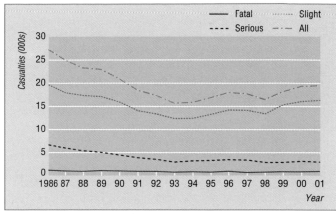
Casualties from road accidents involving illegal alcohol levels 1986-2001

Children and families

If the impact of drink driving is all too obvious, the effect of heavy drinking on families and social networks is much more subtle. One or more problematic drinkers in a family can lead to the breakdown of relationships, disharmony, and the neglect, and in some cases abuse, of children. Such situations are twice as likely to end in divorce: a third of petitions for divorce cite excessive drinking by a partner as a contributory factor. Parents who drink heavily may have an impact on their children's mental wellbeing, educational attainment, and ability to develop normal friendships, not least because their time may be spent looking after a parent or they avoid bringing friends home to prevent embarrassment. A range of surveys suggest that 30-60% of child protection cases involve alcohol.

The relationship between teenagers and alcohol is particularly fraught. The amount of alcohol consumed by children of school age on each drinking occasion doubled during the 1990s, increasing the likelihood of accidents or engagement in risky behaviour—notably unsafe sex. Although alcohol frequently may be used in a planned, as well as unplanned, way to aid the instigation of sexual behaviour because it lowers inhibitions or offers an excuse, the failure to use contraception is more frequently an unplanned and unwanted consequence of drinking. Other consequences of children's drinking may be exclusion from school, truancy, and dropping out.

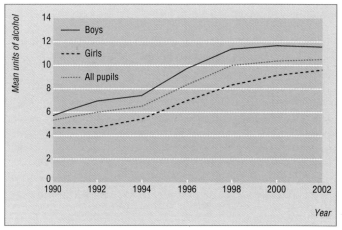
Mean alcohol consumption by school children who had drunk over the past week, by sex, 1990-2001

A relatively small but highly visible impact of alcohol misuse lies with homeless people and street drinkers; the government's Rough Sleepers Unit found that 50% of rough sleepers were dependent on alcohol. Heavy drinking may be a cause of and response to homelessness. With few facilities available to this group, problems can become entrenched, which leads to deterioration in other aspects of health and mental wellbeing.

The politics of alcohol

The ability to tackle alcohol related problems requires the will and resources to do so. The economic arguments are compelling. In addition to the £1.7 billion costs to the NHS and the £12 billion impact of alcohol related crime, a further burden on industry in the United Kingdom results from lost productivity through sickness absence, inability to work, and premature death or retirement. Each year, up to 17 million working days are lost because of alcohol related sickness absence, and productivity is compromised by "sickness presence," in which functioning in the workplace is impaired by a hangover or other effects of excessive drinking. Estimates by the Cabinet Office put the costs to industry of lost productivity at £6.4 billion.

Total costs of around £20 billion make a strong case for investment to tackle the problem of alcohol misuse. Yet in 2001, just £95 million—from a wide range of mostly local

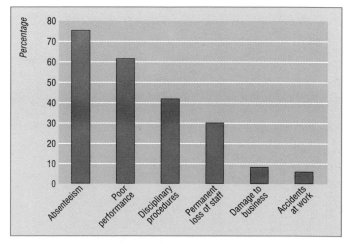
Percentage of employers who attributed selected problems in the workplace to misuse of alcohol

5

sources—was spent on alcohol treatment and little or nothing on preventive campaigns. Set against this is the more than £200 million spent by the drinks industry in advertising their products (or £800 million when all forms of promotion are taken into account). Not only does the alcohol industry have money to spend glamorising and encouraging alcohol consumption, it also is responsible for a £30 billion sector of the economy that delivers about £7 billion a year to the Treasury in excise duties.

Politically, alcohol is a complex and difficult subject. Within government, at least 10 different departments have an interest in alcohol policy, many in direct conflict as to whether to encourage or inhibit the sale and consumption of alcohol. Perhaps not surprising, therefore, is that over the years, problems have been ignored in favour of less prevalent and less damaging—but also less sensitive—issues. Even when the government acknowledged the strength of the arguments for concerted action in 1998 and committed itself to an overarching strategy to tackle the problem, this was followed by further years of inaction, with the excuse that interfering with a popular activity such as drinking would be seen as "nannying" and an unacceptable intervention in an individual's leisure activities. This despite the impact that alcohol demonstrably had on public expenditure and on the ability to access, and make the most of, health service resources.

That change in alcohol policy happens not because of sustained, logical arguments but as a result of random events has been a historical feature over recent decades, with widespread publicity given to particular examples of outrageous behaviour. From the football hooligans of the 1970s to the lager louts of the 1980s and the drunken excesses of young 21st century British holidaymakers in the Mediterranean, governments have waited for examples of clearly unacceptable behaviour to come to public attention before grasping the nettle of alcohol policy. In 2002, the prime minister asked the Strategy Unit in the Cabinet Office to develop a national alcohol harm reduction strategy. Implementation of the strategy—and the impact that it has—will continue to depend on the balancing of economic costs and benefits, pressures on public services and pressures from industry, and political rationale and political expediency.

The figures in this chapter have been adapted from Cabinet Office Strategy Unit. *Alcohol misuse: how much does it cost?* London: Cabinet Office Strategy Unit, 2003.

The drinks industry is directly responsible for employing 50 000 people and indirectly helps generate up to 1 million jobs

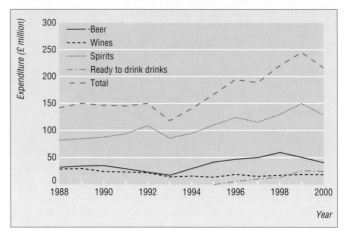

Spending on advertising in the United Kingdom at 2004 prices

Further reading

- Babor T, Caetano R, Casswell S, Edwards G, Giesbrecht N, Graham K, et al. *Alcohol: no ordinary commodity.* Oxford: Oxford University Press, 2003
- Cabinet Office Strategy Unit. *Alcohol harm reduction strategy for England,* March 2004, www.strategy.gov.uk
- Cabinet Office Strategy Unit. *Alcohol misuse: how much does it cost?* London: Cabinet Office Strategy Unit, 2003
- Cooper DB, ed. *Alcohol use.* Oxford: Radcliffe, 2000
- Deehan A. *Alcohol and crime. Taking stock.* London: Home Office, 1999
- Edwards G. *Alcohol. The ambiguous molecule.* London: Penguin, 2000
- Raistrick D, Hodgson R, Ritson B. *Tackling alcohol together. The evidence base for a UK alcohol policy.* London: Free Association Books, 1999

3 Alcohol in the body

Alex Paton

Alcohol (ethanol) is a drug, and health professionals should know something of its physiological and pathological effects and its handling by the body. It is a small, water soluble molecule that is relatively slowly absorbed from the stomach, more rapidly absorbed from the small intestine, and freely distributed throughout the body. Rate of absorption depends on a number of factors: it is quickest, for example, when alcohol is drunk on an empty stomach and the concentration of alcohol is 20-30%. Thus, sherry, with an alcohol concentration of about 20% increases the levels of alcohol in blood more rapidly than beer (3-8%), while spirits (40%) delay gastric emptying and inhibit absorption. Drinks aerated with carbon dioxide—for example, whisky and soda and champagne—get into the system quicker. Food, and particularly carbohydrates, retards absorption: blood concentrations may not reach a quarter of those achieved on an empty stomach. The pleasurable effects of alcohol are best achieved with a meal or when alcohol is drunk diluted in the case of spirits.

Alcoholic drinks are a major source of calories: for example, six pints of beer contain about 500 kcal and half a litre of whisky contains 1650 kcal. The daily energy requirement for a moderately active man is 3000 kcal and for a woman 2200 kcal.

Alcohol is distributed throughout the water in the body, so that most tissues—such as the heart, brain, and muscles—are exposed to the same concentration of alcohol as the blood. The exception is the liver, where exposure is greater because blood is received direct from the stomach and small bowel via the portal vein. Alcohol diffuses rather slowly, except into organs with a rich blood supply such as the brain and lungs. Very little alcohol enters fat because of the latter's poor solubility, so blood and tissue concentrations are higher in women, who have more subcutaneous fat and a smaller blood volume, than in men, even when the amount of alcohol consumed is adjusted for body weight. Women also may have lower levels of alcohol dehydrogenases in the stomach than men, so that less alcohol is metabolised before absorption. Alcohol enters the fetus readily through the placenta and is eliminated by maternal metabolism.

Blood alcohol concentration varies according to sex, size and body build, phase of the menstrual cycle (it is highest premenstrually and at ovulation), previous exposure to alcohol, type of drink, whether alcohol is taken with food or drugs such as cimetidine (which inhibits gastric alcohol dehydrogenase) and antihistamines, phenothiazines, and metoclopramide (which enhance gastric emptying, thus increasing absorption).

Metabolism of alcohol

More than 90% of alcohol is eliminated by the liver; 2-5% is excreted unchanged in urine, sweat, or breath. The first step in metabolism is oxidation by alcohol dehydrogenases (ADH), of which at least four isoenzymes exist, to acetaldehyde in the presence of cofactors (see figure). In healthy people, nearly all of the acetaldehyde, a highly reactive and toxic substance, is oxidised rapidly by aldehyde dehydrogenases (ALDH) to harmless acetate. Several isoenzymes of ALDH exist, one of which is missing in about 50% of Japanese people and possibly other south Asian people (but unusually in Caucasians). Unpleasant symptoms of headache, nausea, flushing, and tachycardia are experienced by people who lack aldehyde dehydrogenases and who drink; this is believed to be because of accumulation of acetaldehyde. Under normal circumstances,

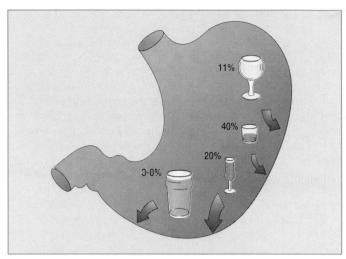

Rate of absorption of alcohol depends on a number of factors: it is quickest when drunk on an empty stomach and the concentration of alcohol is between 20 and 30%

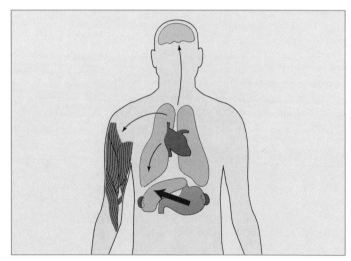

Alcohol is distributed throughout the body water, so that most tissues, such as heart, brain, and muscles, are exposed to the same concentration as in the blood

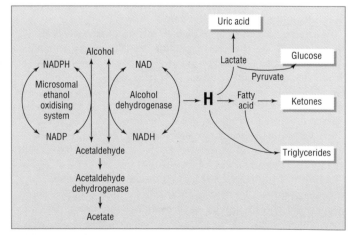

Metabolism of ethanol

acetate is oxidised in liver and peripheral tissues to carbon dioxide and water.

On an empty stomach, blood alcohol concentration peaks about one hour after consumption, depending on the amount drunk; it then declines in a more or less linear manner for the next four hours. Alcohol is removed from the blood at a rate of about 15 mg/100 ml/hour, but this varies in different people, on different drinking occasions, and with the amount of alcohol drunk. At a blood alcohol concentration of 20 mg/100 ml, the curve flattens out, but detectable levels are present for several hours after three pints of beer or three double whiskies in healthy people; enough alcohol to impair normal functioning could be present the morning after an evening session of drinking. Alcohol consumption by heavy drinkers represents a considerable metabolic load: for example, half a bottle of whisky is equivalent in molar terms to 500 g aspirin or 1.2 kg tetracycline.

Two mechanisms dispose of excess alcohol in heavy drinkers and account for "tolerance" in established drinkers. Firstly, normal metabolism increases, as shown by high blood levels of acetate. Secondly, the microsomal ethanol oxidising system is brought into play; this is dependent on P450 cytochrome, normally responsible for drug metabolism, and other cofactors. This is called "enzyme induction" and is produced by other drugs that are metabolised by the liver, and by smoking.

The two mechanisms lead to a redox state, in which free hydrogen ions, which have to be disposed of by a number of alternative pathways, build up. Some of the resultant metabolic aberrations can have clinical consequences: hepatic gluconeogenesis is inhibited, the citric acid cycle is reduced, and oxidation of fatty acids is impaired. Glucose production thus is reduced, with the risk of hypoglycaemia, overproduction of lactic acid blocks uric acid excretion by the kidneys, and accumulated fatty acids are converted into ketones and lipids (see figure showing metabolism of alcohol on previous page).

Behavioural effects

Alcohol is a sedative and mild anaesthetic that is believed to activate the pleasure or reward centres in the brain by triggering release of neurotransmitters such as dopamine and serotonin. It produces a sense of wellbeing, relaxation, disinhibition, and euphoria. These are accompanied by physiological changes such as flushing, sweating, tachycardia, and increases in blood pressure, probably because of stimulation of the hypothalamus and increased release of sympathomimetic amines and pituitary-adrenal hormones. The kidneys secrete more urine, not only because of the fluid drunk but also because of the osmotic effect of alcohol and inhibition of secretion of antidiuretic hormone (ADH).

Increasing consumption leads to a state of **intoxication**, which depends on the amount drunk and previous experience of drinking. Even at a low blood alcohol concentration of around 30 mg/100 ml (6.5 mmol/l), the risk of accidental injury is higher than in the absence of alcohol, although individual experience and complexity of task have to be taken into account. In a simulated driving test, for example, bus drivers with a blood alcohol concentration of 50 mg/100 ml (10.9 mmol/l) thought they could drive through obstacles that were too narrow for their vehicles. At 80 mg/100 ml (17.4 mmol/l)—the current legal limit for driving in this country—the risk of a road accident more than doubles, and at 160 mg/100 ml (34.7 mmol/l), it increases more than 10-fold. People become garrulous, elated, and aggressive at

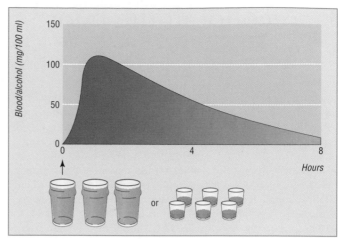

Concentrations of alcohol in the blood after six units of alcohol (see Chapter 4)

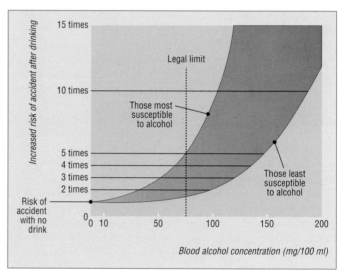

Effect of alcohol on behaviour

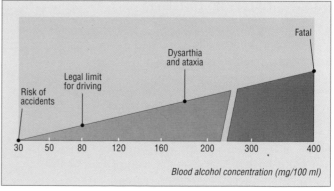

Risks associated with concentrations of alcohol in the blood

levels >100 mg/100 ml (21.7 mmol/l) and then may stop drinking as drowsiness supervenes. After-effects ("hangover") include insomnia, nocturia, tiredness, nausea, and headache. If drinking continues, slurred speech and unsteadiness are likely at around 200 mg/100 ml (43.4 mmol/l), and loss of consciousness may result. Concentrations >400 mg/100 ml (86.8 mmol/l) commonly are fatal as a result of ventricular fibrillation, respiratory failure, or inhalation of vomit (this is particularly likely when drugs have been taken in addition to alcohol).

The figure showing the metabolism of ethanol is adapted from Lieber CS et al. *N Engl J Med.* 1978;298:356. The figure showing the effect of alcohol on behaviour is adapted from Transport and Road Research Laboratory. *The facts about drinking and driving.* Crowthorne: Berkshire, 1983. The figure showing concentrations of alcohol in the blood in heavy, social, and naive drinkers is constructed from figures supplied by Lewis K. *BMJ* 1987;295:800-1.

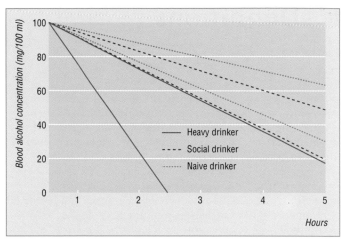

Rate of decrease of concentrations of alcohol in the blood in heavy, social, and naive drinkers

---

Further reading

- Lewis KO. Back calculation of blood alcohol concentration. *BMJ* 1987;295:800-1
- Lieber CS, Salaspuro MP. Alcoholic liver disease. In: Millward-Sadler CHM, Wright R, Arthur MJP, eds. *Wright's liver and biliary disease*, 3rd edn. London: Saunders, 1992:899-964
- Paton A. The body and its health. In: Cooper DB, ed. *Alcohol use.* Oxford: Radcliffe, 2000:25-38

4 Definitions

Alex Paton

Confused thinking about the use and misuse of alcohol arises from myths that have grown up around drink, disagreement over defining what is healthy drinking and what is harmful, and the belief that any criticism of overindulgence is antialcohol, a threat to personal pleasure, and nobody else's business.

In general, people are embarrassed about discussing their drinking, so health professionals need to acquire "the knowledge" (like taxi drivers) by reading a simple guide that is the map of alcohol in order to be confident in dealing dispassionately and subtly with problems that are more common than even health workers realise.

Alcohol

The name is derived from the Arabic *al-kuhl*, literally meaning "the kohl", the antimony powder used to brighten the eyes; it seems to have been adopted in the Middle Ages to describe the "essence" of distillation, while today "alcohol" in everyday speech indicates intoxicating drinks. Technically though, alcohol refers to a large group of chemicals made up of carbon, hydrogen, and oxygen atoms in the form of a single hydroxyl (OH) group and varying numbers of methyl (CH_2) groups. The simplest are water soluble liquids with only a few carbon atoms, those with perhaps half a dozen or more carbons are oily substances, and the most complex, with up to 20 carbon atoms, are waxes.

Strictly speaking, the alcohol we drink is ethyl alcohol or **ethanol** (a term favoured by north American workers); it has the chemical formula C_2H_5OH. In this chapter, the term "alcohol" will be used in the popular sense, denoting a drink containing ethyl alcohol. Such drinks are produced by two processes:

- **fermentation** by yeast of crushed fruits such as grape wines, or grains such as barley for beer
- **distillation**, in which alcoholic drinks are evaporated to produce spirits.

Alcohol content

For scientific purposes, the amount of alcohol in a drink is best measured in grams (g) of absolute alcohol; this allows comparison across countries. It is unhelpful to talk about "number of drinks," because volume of drink and quantity of alcohol in individual beers, wines, and spirits vary. Some countries have tried to get around the problem by defining a "standard drink" that in theory can be understood by everyone.

In the United Kingdom, one unit is equal to approximately 8 g of absolute alcohol per 10 ml, as is found in half a pint (285 ml) of average strength beer, a glass of wine (125 ml), a small glass of sherry (50 ml), or a "single" of spirits (25 ml).

The formula to calculate units in different types of drink is % alcohol by volume × volume/100 × 10. When an alcohol worker inquires about a person's drinking, it is worth checking details of the amounts, as pubs and restaurants serve drinks that are larger than these standards—and so do people pouring drinks at home.

Although the United Kingdom favours 8 g as the standard drink, the standard in other countries varies from 6 g in Ireland, to 10 g in Australasia, 12 g in the United States, and as much as

Myths of alcohol

Myth	Reality
• No one, especially heavy drinkers, tells the truth about their drinking	• Do you know how much you drank last week, or in the pub last Saturday?
• Health workers and their clients and patients are uncomfortable about discussing alcohol	• An excuse for letting untrained health workers, especially doctors, off the hook
• Treatment of alcoholics is a hopeless business	• Most heavy drinkers are not "alcoholics," and two thirds will accept advice from a health professional to cut down

Different alcohols

Chemical name	Molecular formula	Common name	Comment
Methyl alcohol	CH_3OH	Methanol, meths	Can cause blindness
Ethyl alcohol	C_2H_5OH	**Ethanol**	The alcohol we drink
Amyl alcohol	$C_5H_{11}OH$		Oily
Cetyl alcohol	$C_{16}H_{35}OH$		Waxy, spermaceti
Melissyl alcohol	$C_{20}H_{41}OH$		Beeswax

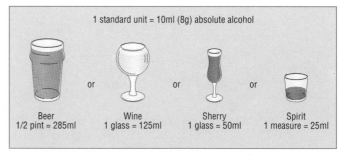

Drinks equivalent to one, or one and a half, units (12% wine) of alcohol

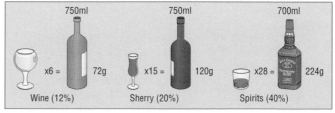

Number of glasses per bottle of different drinks

20 g in Japan. Three "drinks" a day in Japan would be well into hazardous levels in the United Kingdom.

The alcohol content of individual beers varies from 3% to 8%, of wines from 10% to 20%, and of spirits from 40% to 60%. Strong lagers may contain four units per 330 ml can (equal to two pints of beer) and alcopops mostly contain 4-5.5% alcohol, while some designer drinks enjoyed by the young contain 8-20% alcohol; the alcohol in many of these is disguised by the fruit flavour.

Sensible drinking

No such thing exists as a completely safe level of drinking; only teetotallers run no risk. A few particularly sensitive people—women more often than men—find that they are made ill by small quantities of alcohol; this may be a true hypersensitivity or perhaps because of an inborn defect of an enzyme such as acetaldehyde dehydrogenase (see Chapter 5). Blood pressure rises with each unit of alcohol, even with social drinking, although this probably is physiological and harmless. More alarming is the modest rise in relative risk (1.5) of breast cancer in women drinking as few as seven units a week; one suggestion is that this may be connected with women drinking under the age of 25 years. Naive (inexperienced) drinkers may become intoxicated and damage themselves or others with relatively small amounts of alcohol.

At the end of the 1980s, the then Health Education Council and a consensus of the medical Royal Colleges established a sensible (low risk) level of 21 units a week for men and 14 units a week for women. The government in the United Kingdom later refined these figures by recommending a **daily** intake of not more than four units for men and three units for women, with two alcohol free days a week, in order to avoid people drinking large amounts on one or more occasion even though remaining within weekly limits.

Alcohol misuse

Somewhere under 10% of people in the United Kingdom do not drink alcohol at all and 80% are social drinkers. A minority of up to 15% drink more than sensible levels: figures produced by the government in 2003 suggest 9 million people in England do so. These people are best described as **misusing** (not abusing) alcohol; no longer is it acceptable to call such people "alcoholics" or to label misuse as "alcoholism." The first term is stigmatising and the second implies the existence of a disease called alcoholism. Although the latter still may be a popular concept in the United States, the consensus in the United Kingdom is that a spectrum exists from no drinking to dependency, and that people are capable of passing from one stage to another in either direction in the course of their lives. Very rarely, even dependent drinkers have been known to return to "comfortable" drinking. Scottish experts recently suggested that the phrase "the problems some people have with alcohol" is less judgmental than "misusing alcohol."

Despite claims for and against different types of drink, what matters is not what is drunk but how much **ethanol**, although factors such as constitution, sex, social background, occupation, diet, and, above all, reasons for drinking must be taken into account. In general, the younger a person starts drinking regularly, the more likely they will have problems and the earlier they will arise, and, in general, women are more sensitive than men. Generalisation about how much and for how long any one person has to drink before trouble starts is not possible. Two examples make this clear. Firstly, people aged 18-24 years are notorious for their capacity to drink, yet most will moderate

Types of drinking

Type	Definition
Sensible	Women 3 units, men 4 units a day with two alcohol free days, or women 14 units, men 21 units a week
Social moderate	As above with occasional drinking over sensible levels
Naive	Infrequent drinker, sensitive to overindulgence
Heavy	Persistent drinking above sensible levels
Hazardous	*Risk* of harm at levels around 6 units for women and 8 units for men a day (WHO)
Binge	Drinking double sensible levels or more on a single occasion
Harmful problem	*Presence* of social or physical harm or problems caused at levels around 6 units for women and 8 units a day for men (WHO)
Dependent	Addiction to alcohol

> Social drinking can therefore be defined as drinking within sensible levels

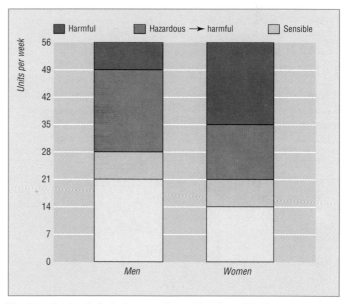

Number of units of alcohol per week considered sensible, hazardous to harmful, and harmful

> Alcohol misuse is a convenient shorthand to indicate repeated, excessive consumption of alcohol that can lead to problem drinking—85% of which involves social, economic, moral, or psychological difficulties and 15% physical damage or dependence (addiction)

their drinking in later years, largely because of lifestyle pressures, without coming to harm. Secondly, some people can drink heavily all their lives and still function successfully.

Heavy drinking may be used as a catch all for several varieties of drinking more than sensible levels:

- Binge drinking
- Hazardous drinking
- Harmful drinking.

To these definitions should be added **social harm**, which is perhaps the most important danger of alcohol misuse, to emphasise that it is not just the drinker who suffers—family, friends, and even strangers also are affected. An average of six people are said to be affected by a problem drinker.

The **dependent (addicted drinker)** has a high daily intake of alcohol and is totally unable to stop. Physical features of shakes, sweating, and nausea combine with psychological symptoms of compulsion, craving, and anxiety to keep the drinking going, so that it overrides all other activities. A drink first thing in the morning to relieve the shakes is characteristic; if alcohol cannot be obtained, withdrawal symptoms, including delirium tremens, are likely.

Skid row drinker is the term used for people who have been taken over by alcohol to the extent that he (less often she) is down and out, lives rough, and begs or steals to finance the habit. The name is derived from a sloping area of Seattle where logs used to be rolled into Puget Sound.

The amounts of alcohol that are potentially harmful are impossible to predict because of individual variation in sensitivity, but regarding continued consumption of 35 units a week (five units a day) by men and 28 units a week (four units a day) by women as risky is reasonable. The World Health Organization gives eight or more units a day for men and six or more units a day for women as the usual level associated with all types of heavy drinking, but this does not mean that lesser amounts are safe.

Features of alcohol dependence

- Drinking more than 10 units daily
- Tolerance to alcohol: blood alcohol levels greater than 150 mg/100ml without drunkenness
- Repeated withdrawal symptoms; morning shakes relieved by alcohol
- Repertoire narrowed by drink
- Compulsion to drink in spite of problems
- Abnormal laboratory tests

Further reading

- Morgan MY, Ritson EB. *Alcohol and health. A handbook for students and medical practitioners.* London: Medical Council on Alcohol, 2003
- Saunders JB, Aasland OG, Amundsen A, Grant M. Alcohol consumption and related problems among primary care patients: WHO collaborative project on early detection of persons with harmful alcohol consumption–I. *Addiction* 1993;88:349-62

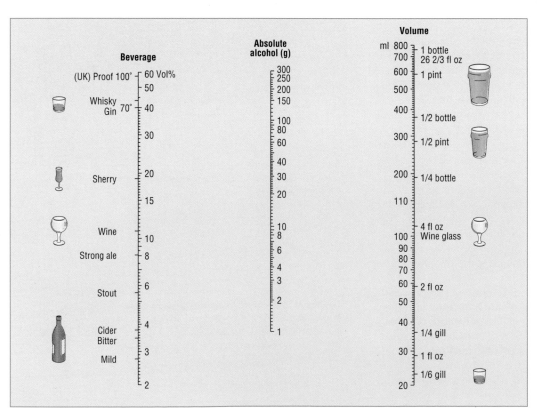

Calculating the amount of absolute alcohol in a drink. Adapted from Mellor CS. *BMJ* 1970;iii:703

5 Nature of alcohol use

Alex Paton

Most people enjoy alcohol and drink sensibly, with occasional lapses—usually when they are young or during celebrations. The pattern of drinking may vary during life, being heaviest in young adulthood, then moderate, and possibly heavier again later in life, as prosperity and responsibility increase. The capacity to switch between categories is important: the nature of a person's drinking should not necessarily be regarded as immutable, although a regular pattern sometimes is established by middle age. Regular drinking does not necessarily progress through habit and tolerance to heavier drinking and then dependence; even persistently heavy drinkers may escape harm.

Mechanisms underlying drinking

Some people are vulnerable and others are not: the interaction of a person with alcohol results from a complicated mixture of influences that determine not only drinking response but also outcome in terms of social, psychological, and physical effects. Our understanding of the mechanisms involved is limited.

Genes

Early research showed greater concordance of "alcoholism" in monozygotic (identical) twins than dizygotic (non-identical) twins, and a fourfold increase in "alcoholism" among men adopted away from alcoholic parents soon after birth. Initial enthusiasm for an important genetic factor, however, has been tempered by problems with research methods, conflicting results, and problems defining "alcoholism", although, recently, identical twins were shown to develop cirrhosis three times more often than dizygotic twins.

Genes probably play a minor role in the generality of alcohol misuse; a compromise might be that biological factors predispose and environmental factors determine. To suggest that different genes will be shown to control different aspects of the alcohol "syndrome"—for example, ability to tolerate different amounts of drink, susceptibility to toxic metabolites, sensitivity to end organ damage, and dependence—is tempting. Clearer definitions than currently used terms like heavy drinking, alcoholism, and even alcohol misuse will be needed.

Family

Up to 50% of heavy drinkers have a family history of alcohol misuse: they are characterised by being men, starting to drink young, chaotic drinking, frequently becoming addicted, and antisocial behaviour. Subtle physiological and psychological changes in response to alcohol have been shown in enzyme activity and brain waves in sons from alcoholic families, but environment probably still is stronger than genes.

Constitution

Low self-esteem; lack of education, interests, and skills; boredom, habit, loneliness; anxiety, and depression (with a relative risk of 1.7) are some triggers that promote drinking.

Environment

Most drinking is determined by:

- Culture, customs and attitudes
- Availability and price
- Individual needs and responses
- Life events and circumstances

Alcohol can harm bodies, minds, families, societies, and economies

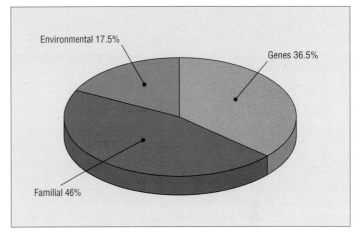

Influences on risk of misusing alcohol

Influences on drinking patterns

- Genetic (biochemical)
- Familial (biological)
- Constitutional (behavioural)
- Environmental

Proposed genetic mechanisms behind drinking behaviour

Aldehyde dehydrogenase deficiency
- The well known aldehyde dehydrogenase deficiency, inherited as an autosomal dominant in Oriental populations, is a single genetic mechanism that affects drinking behaviour.
- This seems to be a special case. A search of polymorphisms of alcohol dehydrogenase has not shown any particular genetic influence on drinking behaviour in general.

Abnormal immune response
- Susceptibility to liver damage was suggested to be the result of an abnormal immune response that is genetically determined, but this would apply to a rather special group of heavy drinkers.

A1 allele of D2 dopamine receptor gene
- Great interest has been aroused by reports that severe "alcoholics" are significantly more likely to carry the A1 allele of the D2 dopamine receptor gene as a marker than controls with normal drinking patterns.
- These findings were based on brain samples taken post-mortem and might have resulted from alcohol damage rather than a genetic cause of "alcoholism"; they have not always been confirmed by other workers, so the jury is still out.

- Occupation
- Difficulty adapting to unfamiliar environments.

Patterns of drinking

Alcohol drinking is determined by social structure, demography, and religious and ethical attitudes. A simple illustration of this is the well known difference between the British who drink in pubs and the people of Mediterranean countries who drink alcohol with meals. In the United Kingdom, more money is spent on alcohol than on any other commodity. For most people, drink is a source of pleasure, because it is sociable, relatively cheap, and comforting. Drink is also a substantial producer of wealth for the country, yet problems resulting from misuse come near to destroying the financial benefits. According to figures from the government's alcohol strategy unit in 2003, the £30 billion industry from which it benefits to the tune of £7 billion in taxes is offset by the £20 billion cost of the damage done by alcohol. The trade off between wealth and health, rather than any anti-alcohol stance as trumpeted by media and drinks industry, should determine what action against misuse we are prepared to accept.

Alcohol consumption per head (capita) of population in England is currently around nine litres; this has risen recently, after being steady at seven litres for the last 10 years. On average, men drink 16 units of alcohol a week and women 5.4 units. Beer still accounts for more than half (54%) of the alcohol drunk in the United Kingdom, although its share of the market has declined over the past 20 years as wine (21%) and spirits (20%) have increased in popularity, especially among women. Similar trends are reported in other industrialised countries. Patterns of drinking vary in different groups of the population, and some of these need to be considered separately.

Children

Although the legal age for drinking in the United Kingdom is 18 years (compared with 21 years in the United States), the average age at which children start drinking is 10-11 in both sexes. Ninety per cent of children have tasted alcohol by the age of 15, and half report having been drunk on occasion. The average amount consumed by children aged 10-15 has doubled since 1990 to 10 units a week; Welsh children head the European league table of young consumers. Although a quarter of children aged 14 and nearly all those aged 17 drink illegally in pubs, underage drinking is permitted in registered youth clubs, and for children to drink anywhere but in a pub from the age of five is not illegal.

People aged 16-24 years

Peak rates of drinking occur at this time. In 2000, 41% of men and 33% of women in this age group drank above sensible limits compared with 29% and 19%, respectively, in older age groups. Compulsive drinking is a feature in this group, with two out of five people admitting to regular binge drinking.

Women

The most striking social change in drinking in the last 30 years has been the enormous popularity of drinking among women. In general, although women drink less and more moderately than men, they are more sensitive to equivalent amounts of alcohol. Younger women, however, especially professionals, increasingly resemble men in their use of alcohol, although with a preference for spirits or wine over beer. The result has been a marked increase in the numbers of women who drink more than sensible levels (which is set to continue), social problems arising earlier and after a shorter time than in men, and more

Environmental influences

Culture, customs and attitudes
- No drinking by strict Muslims
- Jews on the whole abstain from heavy drinking

Availability and price
- In the United Kingdom, drink can be obtained from many sources other than pubs and off licences at almost any time of day or night, for example, supermarkets, garages, trains, ships and aircraft
- In spite of the impost on alcohol, its price has always been cheap in relation to cost of living indices

Individual needs and responses
- Individual need for fellowship or risk taking
- Responses to peer pressure, particularly among the young, competitive lifestyle

Life events and circumstances
- Loss of a job
- Divorce
- Bereavement
- Loneliness, such as the lonely housewife

Occupation
- Stressful occupations or those where alcohol is readily available; some individuals may be unconsciously attracted to the latter
- Standardised mortality rates for cirrhosis of the liver are particularly high among publicans and others in the catering trades, seamen, members of the armed services, and airline pilots

Difficulty in adapting to an alien environment
- Asians, for example, who may not have touched alcohol before moving to a culture in which alcohol is freely available, may be particularly vulnerable

Adolescents' drinking activities are part of the risk taking and peer pressure of growing up, and most will reduce their drinking as their responsibilities increase

"Don't follow me in here, Dad — pubs aren't a suitable place for blokes"

physical damage. Twenty years ago, for example, the ratio of men to women who developed cirrhosis was 5:1; this now is approaching 1:1. These trends have implications for alcohol services, which have traditionally been male orientated. (For drinking in pregnancy see Chapter 8.)

Older people

Scant attention has been paid to drinking in older people: around half of those in contact with health workers are never questioned about their alcohol intake. Where surveys have been done, 11-33% of older people were drinking more than sensible levels of alcohol, but this had been recognised in less than one quarter. Older people's common practice of adding alcohol to tea or coffee is not always appreciated; when specifically asked about this, the number of heavy drinkers doubled.

Alcohol misuse may be difficult to disentangle from illness and can be missed because symptoms are attributed to old age. Removal from a familiar environment may result in confusion because of alcohol withdrawal rather than simple disorientation, in which case a small glass of sherry or whisky can be a useful therapeutic test.

Drinking may be caused by loneliness, lack of support and stimulation, insomnia, or anxiety and depression, and steps to improve social functioning may be fruitful. Recommended sensible levels may need to be reduced for older patients. American experts, for example, recommend not more than one standard drink (1.5 units) a day, but care should be taken not to condemn drinking unless it is clearly out of control; alcohol may be one of the few comforts left.

Statistics of misuse

According to government statistics, 9.1 million people in England (with a population in round figures of 50 million) drink more than sensible levels. One in three men and one in five women in Britain are claimed to drink more than sensible levels; this is twice the number 20 years ago.

Any statistics about alcohol consumption should be regarded as approximate, because people do not always accurately report their drinking habits, and one survey uncovered less than half the consumption known from sales of alcohol. We have little information on the amount of home production of alcohol or imports from the Continent (legal or illegal). Comparisons also are complicated by the use of different denominators: per capita consumption in those aged >15 years or in the whole population and figures for the United Kingdom, England and Wales or for England only.

Given these provisos, if 9 million people are accepted to be drinking above sensible levels, more than half will be drinking hazardously, 2-3 million will be having problems (drinking harmfully), and up to one tenth or 900 000 could be dependent on alcohol. Translating this into a general practice with an average of 2000 patients per partner: 360 patients would be drinking more than sensible levels; half of these would be hazardous drinkers, perhaps 100 would be having problems, and 36 would be dependent. Surveys have shown repeatedly that only a small proportion of these are known to the practice.

> By asking questions, practice staff are in a position not only to take action at a stage when misuse of alcohol is treatable but can also provide much needed information about the amount and type of drinking in the population

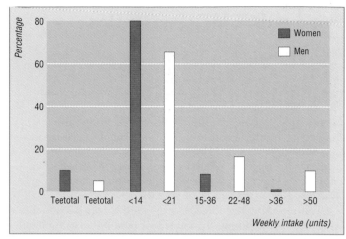

Distribution of alcohol intake among men and women

Warning signs of alcohol misuse in older patients

- Frequent falls
- Incontinence
- Malnutrition
- Hypothermia
- Confusion

People	Numbers	
	Population (50 million)	General practice (2000 patients per partner)
Drinking above sensible levels	9 million	360
Heavy drinkers	4.5 million	180
Problem drinkers	2-3 million	80-120
Dependent drinkers	900 000	36

Drinking and harm

- Many heavy and problem drinkers do not seek help because they do not admit that their drinking is harmful
- Many people are harmed by somebody else's drinking but are reluctant to seek help for fear of offending the drinker
- Serious physical damage and dependence are nearly always irreversible
- Health workers should concentrate on detecting heavy and problem drinkers for whom advice and information about sensible drinking—"brief intervention"—is likely not only to be successful but to cost little in time, resources and money

Further reading

- Marshall EJ, Murray RM. The familial transmission of alcoholism. *BMJ* 1991;303:72-3
- O'Connell H, Chin A-V, Cunningham C, Lawlor B. Alcohol use disorders in elderly people—redefining an age old problem in old age. *BMJ* 2003;327:664-7
- Plant M. *Women and alcohol: contemporary and historical perspectives*. London: Free Association Books, 1997
- Royal College of Physicians, British Paediatric Society. *Alcohol and the young*. London: Royal College of Physicians, 1995

6 Detecting misuse

Alex Paton

Asking the right questions

Many people, not least health professionals, find it difficult to quiz people about their drinking for a number of reasons. Even so, most people who drink heavily give answers that tally with information from other sources (useful corroboration when available), and if amounts are regarded as approximate, valuable information can be obtained.

Health workers need to overcome their reluctance to talk about alcohol by gaining the individual's confidence. Sometimes "social" questions may be useful to assess the part alcohol plays in the individual's life. The ideal is to ask questions about alcohol and record the answers whenever a history is taken; the only reason for not doing so is when an individual is incapable of answering. The same neutral, matter of fact manner should be used as with other questions, and it may be best to include questions about alcohol with other questions about lifestyle, such as those about smoking, diet, exercise, and medications, or when discussing symptoms or previous illness that might be relevant. For most people, five questions, which should take no more than a minute to ask, will suffice:

- Do you drink alcohol?
- When did you start drinking?
- What do you drink?
- How much do you drink?
- How often do you drink?

If the individual does not drink, reasons should be sought; these may be abstention because of temperance or religious beliefs, a result of former misuse, or sometimes to cover up for perceived shame about heavy drinking. Do not be put off by people who say they used to drink heavily but no longer do. "Not much" is not an acceptable answer. If heavy drinking is suspected, one technique is to ask if they drink a deliberately high amount—for example, 30 pints of beer or a bottle of whisky a day—and then to reduce the amount as necessary. The approximate level can be gauged by the individual's reaction. **Never** ask whether an individual is or has been an alcoholic; this almost certainly will be resented because of the stigma, which likely will conflict with their self-image.

Questionnaires

For normal practice, to establish estimates of "quantity" and "frequency" of drinking usually is enough. If more information is needed, it may be best to set aside time for a special interview. Alternatively, self-administered questionnaires can be used to save time. Their disadvantage is that they depend on honest answers from an individual who may be unwilling to admit social problems or police convictions. They lack the subtlety of the clinical interview—no substitute exists for dispassionate face to face discussion—and self-administered questionnaires depend on the patient being well enough and motivated. Questionnaires should be short, simple, and easily understood in everyday language; they can be given to spouses if that is desirable. Interactive questionnaires on computers have the advantage of being impersonal and are said to be particularly reliable with heavier drinkers. They have been validated for a wide range of educational backgrounds and intelligence.

A number of questionnaires have been developed specifically to detect people who misuse alcohol. Where time is at a premium, one of the most effective is the Paddington Alcohol Test, which takes about one minute and was designed for use by

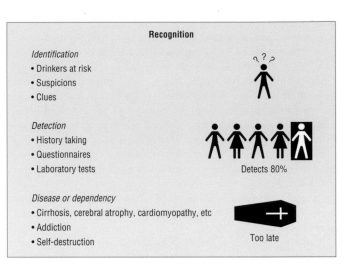

Recognition of people who misuse alcohol

Useful "social" questions to gain people's confidence

- Do you go to the pub after work?
- Do you have a drink with meals?
- Do you go drinking at weekends?

Reasons for reluctance to discuss drinking habits

- Alcohol is an emotional topic and is liable to generate strong feelings
- Reluctance to broach what still is regarded as an intimate matter and therefore taboo
- Suspicion on the part of the client or patient that the questioner may be against alcohol and regard drinking as wrong
- Widely held belief that heavy drinkers in particular will not be honest with their answers
- Lack of knowledge about alcohol and therefore lack of confidence on the part of health workers

---

Include questions about alcohol with other lifestyle questions

Smoking
- Do you smoke?
- What do you smoke?
- How much do you smoke?
- How long have you been smoking?

Drinking
- Do you drink?
- What do you drink?
- Roughly how much do you drink?
- How long have you been drinking?

Medication
- Do you take tablets or medicine?
- What are they for?

doctors and nurses in a busy accident and emergency unit at St Mary's Hospital, London (see Chapter 7). It has been validated over the past 10 years and provides an aide memoir of conditions that should trigger suspicion of alcohol misuse appropriate to such departments, asks four questions, and gives guidance on what action to take. No reason seems to exist why this type of questionnaire should not be adapted to other situations, such as for fracture clinics, genitourinary medicine clinics, and general practice, where screening could be undertaken on registration.

Questionnaires useful for screening for heavy drinking

- Paddington Alcohol Test (PAT)
- Alcohol use disorders identification test (AUDIT)
- Michigan alcoholism screening test (MAST)
- CAGE
- Severity of alcohol dependence questionnaire

PADDINGTON ALCOHOL TEST revised (PAT)
2004
PATIENT IDENTIFICATION STICKER:

Circle number(s) - for specific trigger(s); consider for ALL the **TOP 10**

1. FALL *(i. trip)*	2. COLLAPSE *(i. fits)*	3. HEAD INJURY *(i. facial)*	4. ASSAULT
5. ACCIDENT *(i. Burn, RTA)*	6. UNWELL *(i. Request detox/help, self neglect)*		7. NON-SPECIFIC G.I.
8. PSYCHIATRIC	9. CARDIAC *(i. Chest pain)*	10. REPEAT ATTENDER	Other (specify):-

After dealing with patient's agenda, i.e. patient's reason for attendance:-

1 "We routinely ask all patients in A&E if they drink alcohol - do you drink?"   Yes > 2. (No)

2 "Quite a number of people have times when they drink more than usual; what is the most you will drink in any one day?" *(Pub measures in units; home measures often x3!)*

Beer/lager/cider	___ Pints (2)	___ Cans (1.5)	Total units/day=
Strong beer/lager/cider	___ Pints (5)	___ Cans (4)	
Wine	___ Glasses (1.5)	___ Bottles (9)	
Fortified wine (sherry, Martini)	___ Glasses (1)	___ Bottles (12)	
Spirits (gin, whisky, vodka)	___ Singles (1)	___ Bottles (30)	

3 If this is more than 8 units/day for a man, or 6 units/day for a woman, "Does this happen.......

  : Everyday?   = **PAT +ve** Dependent drinker Y/N (? Pabrinex)

  : At least once a month   = **PAT +ve** Hazardous drinker Y/N

4 "Do you feel your current attendance is related to alcohol?"   **YES** = **PAT +ve** NO = *PAT -ve*

If **PAT +ve**   "We gently advise you this drinking is harming your health"

          "Would you like to see our Health Worker?"   **YES**/NO - give leaflet

Note: "i" = including

Paddington Alcohol Test revised (PAT)

ABC of Alcohol

A questionnaire suitable for screening in primary care is the alcohol use disorders identification test (AUDIT), which was developed by the World Health Organization to detect all varieties of heavy drinking, particularly in people who are drinking hazardously or with early problems, rather than only physically damaged or dependent drinkers. The test is self-administered and consists of 10 questions that relate to consumption (three questions), drinking behaviour and problems (four questions), and dependence (three questions). A score of ≥8 of a possible 40 strongly indicates misuse.

AUDIT

Please circle the answer that is correct for you

1. How often do you have a drink containing alcohol?

| Never | Monthly or less | Two to four times a month | Two to three times a week | Four or more times a week |

2. How many drinks containing alcohol do you have on a typical day when you drinking?

| 1 or 2 | 3 or 4 | 5 or 6 | 7 or 9 | 10 or more |

3. How often do you have six or more drinks on one occasion?

| Never | Less than monthly | Monthly | Weekly | Daily or almost daily |

4. How often during the last year have you found that you were not able to stop drinking once you had started?

| Never | Less than monthly | Monthly | Weekly | Daily or almost daily |

5. How often during the last year have you failed to do what was normally expected from you because of drinking?

| Never | Less than monthly | Monthly | Weekly | Daily or almost daily |

6. How often during the last year have you needed a first drink in the morning to get yourself going after a heavy drinking session?

| Never | Less than monthly | Monthly | Weekly | Daily or almost daily |

7. How often during the last year have you had a feeling of guilt or remorse after drinking?

| Never | Less than monthly | Monthly | Weekly | Daily or almost daily |

8. How often during the last year have you been unable to remember what happened the night before because you had been drinking?

| Never | Less than monthly | Monthly | Weekly | Daily or almost daily |

9. Have you or someone else been injured as a result of your drinking?

| No | | Yes, but not in the last year | | Yes, during the last year |

10. Has a relative or friend, or a doctor or other health worker been concerned about your drinking or suggested you cut down?

| No | | Yes, but not in the last year | | Yes, during the last year |

Procedure for scoring AUDIT

Questions 1-8 are scored 0, 1, 2, 3, or 4. Question 9 and 10 are scored 0, 2 or 4 only. The response coding is as follows:

	0	1	2	3	4
Questions 1	Never	Monthly or less	Two to four times a month	Two to three times a week	Four or more times a week
Questions 2	1 or 2	3 or 4	5 or 6	7 or 9	10 or more
Questions 3-8	Never	Less than monthly	Monthly	Weekly	Daily or almost daily
Questions 9-10	No		Yes, but not in the last year		Yes, during the last year

The minimum score (for non-drinkers) is 0 and the maximum possible score is 40.
A score of 8 or more indicates a strong likelihood of hazardous or harmful alcohol consumption.

Alcohol use disorders identification test (AUDIT)

The alcohol use disorders identification test has superseded the brief Michigan alcoholism screening test (MAST), arguably the most popular questionnaire until now. This also has 10 items that can be self-administered; a score of five or more identifies 98% of "alcoholics"—patients who are physically harmed or dependent—but less than half of those with alcohol problems of a lesser degree. Similar limitations apply to the four questions in the CAGE test: the very nature of which (two or more positive replies are diagnostic) shows that it is targeted at dependent drinkers. To use this instrument to screen people who are mostly at the lower end of the spectrum of alcohol misuse risks alienation of those who could benefit most from advice to cut down on their drinking (brief intervention).

Specialist alcohol units on the other hand may need to assess degrees of dependence, and the self-administered severity of alcohol dependence questionnaire was developed for this purpose. It has a series of 20 questions, each of which has four possible answers: scores of 4-19 indicate mild to moderate dependence and scores of >20 indicate moderate to severe dependence.

Laboratory tests

The suitability of conventional blood tests, such as tests of the liver enzymes aspartate aminotransferase, alanine aminotransferase, and γ glutamyl transferase, and red cell mean corpuscular volume for the diagnosis of alcohol misuse is limited. They mostly have been used to distinguish harmful drinkers from social drinkers, and they are unlikely to detect people with lesser degrees of misuse. No single test, alone or in combination, can give an unequivocal answer. Those that are the most sensitive are not invariably abnormal, and, when results are abnormal, many other causes besides alcohol exist. Such tests are affected by diseases of the liver, blood, heart, and kidneys and by drugs, especially those that "induce" enzyme activity, such as barbiturates, anticonvulsants, and steroid hormones. If these causes can be excluded, mildly abnormal values should raise the possibility of misuse before serious physical damage occurs, when advice about cutting down would be beneficial.

The most sensitive markers are γ glutamyl transferase and mean corpuscular volume; together these identify two thirds of hospital patients who misuse alcohol but only 20-25% of people seen in primary care. The enzyme γ glutamyl transferase "leaks" from the liver into the bloodstream in response to alcohol, and blood levels >40 IU/l are found in 80% of drinkers with physical problems (men and women), but they do not indicate serious liver damage unless levels are in the hundreds. An increase in blood levels of γ glutamyl transferase sometimes can occur after a social drinking session, with levels returning to normal after about 48 hours. Whether this is because of individual sensitivity or the beginning of liver damage is not clear, but such abnormalities should be followed up, as levels are likely to remain high in heavy drinkers.

An increase in size of red blood cells (mean corpuscular volume) from an upper limit of 90 fl is found in about 60% of people who seriously misuse alcohol; it is more common in women than men. This increase can be the result of a direct toxic action of alcohol on the bone marrow, dietary deficiency of folic acid, or liver damage. If causes other than alcohol can be excluded—and again many exist—a high mean corpuscular volume is particularly meaningful, because the action of alcohol on developing red blood cells differs from its effect on liver enzymes. The mean corpuscular volume takes up to three months to return to normal after abstinence, reflecting turnover of red cells by the bone marrow.

CAGE
- Have you ever felt you ought to **cut down** on your drinking?
- Have people **annoyed** you by criticizing your drinking?
- Have you ever felt bad or **guilty** about your drinking?
- Have you ever had a drink first thing in the morning to steady your nerves or get rid of a hangover: **eye-opener**?

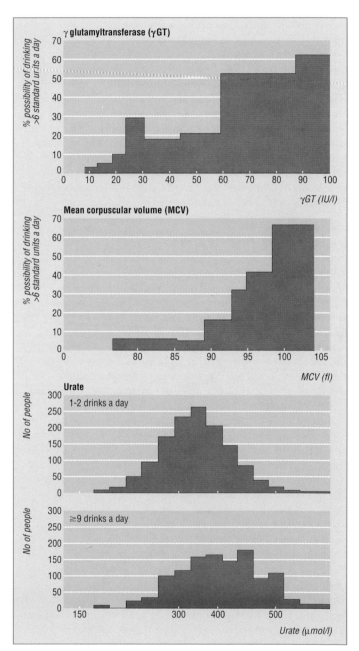

Laboratory markers of alcohol misuse

Combined measurement of γ glutamyl transferase and mean corpuscular volume is a cheap and simple way of detecting heavy drinking in routine practice, although normal values do not, of course, rule out the possibility that a person is drinking heavily. Increasing concentrations of each marker can be related to increasing alcohol intake, but again they give only a statistical probability of misuse. In spite of these caveats, distribution of blood levels, especially of γ glutamyl transferase, in the general population is heavily skewed towards the lower end; values in the upper range of normal should be viewed with suspicion, particularly if another marker is abnormal.

Supportive evidence may sometimes be obtained from high blood levels of uric acid, fasting triglycerides (which give the serum a milky colour), aspartate aminotransferase, and alanine aminotransferase. Uric acid and triglyceride levels are high in about half of heavy drinking men but are poor discriminators in women. Levels of urea in the blood sometimes are reduced in heavy drinkers because alcohol inhibits enzymes in the urea cycle. A high ratio of aspartate aminotransferase to alanine aminotransferase may suggest alcohol misuse, but the levels of these enzymes are likely to be abnormal in other types of liver damage. So far, no evidence shows that newer, and often more expensive, blood tests—such as carbohydrate deficient transferrin (desialotransferrin), glutathione transferase, or mitochondrial aspartate aminotransferase—offer any significant advantage over currently used tests.

Alcohol levels

Blood

Estimates of the blood alcohol concentration are not used enough to detect misuse of alcohol. Such levels can be measured in toxicology laboratories and in many chemical pathology departments. High levels can provide incontrovertible evidence of drinking, and, because alcohol is eliminated relatively slowly from the blood, appreciable amounts may be found for 24 hours after a drinking session. Problem drinkers who have developed tolerance may have blood alcohol concentrations that do not reflect the extent of their drinking.

A blood alcohol concentration that exceeds 80 mg/100 ml (17.4 mmol/l)—the legal limit for driving in the United Kingdom—especially in the morning is highly suggestive of alcohol misuse, and levels >150 mg/100 ml (32.5 mmol/l) are diagnostic. They do not distinguish an isolated drinking bout from chronic alcohol misuse, but if the individual shows no signs of inebriation at a concentration ≥80 mg, they can be assumed to be a heavy drinker. Estimates of blood alcohol concentration should always be considered in unconscious patients: values usually exceed 300 mg/100 ml (65.1 mmol/l) if alcohol alone is responsible.

Breath

Levels of alcohol in the breath accurately reflect the levels in the blood (correlation 0.96), are simple to test with an alcolmeter, and provide an immediate result. The individual is told to take a deep breath and blow out into the instrument. An end expiratory air sample is analysed on the principle that oxygen in breath converts alcohol in the presence of a catalyst into water and carbon dioxide. The chemical energy released is converted into an electrical charge proportional to the amount of alcohol in the sample. A value of 35 μg/100 ml is equivalent to a level of alcohol in the blood of 80 mg/100 ml. Mouthwashes and the presence of diabetes may give false positive results, and people with chronic lung disease may fail to produce an adequate air sample. Several varieties of alcolmeter are available, and they can be used with minimal instruction. One instrument (Lion,

Conventional tests: no unequivocal abnormal values

Test for	Normal value
γ Glutamyl transferase	<40 IU/l
Mean corpuscular volume	<85 fl
Urate	120-360 μmol/l
Fasting triglycerides	0.85-2 mmol/l
Aspartate aminotransferase	<25 IU/l
Alanine aminotransferase	<21 IU/l

Concentrations of alcohol per 100 ml

Blood (mg)	Breath (μg)	Urine (mg)
50	22	67
80	35	107
150	66	200
250	110	333

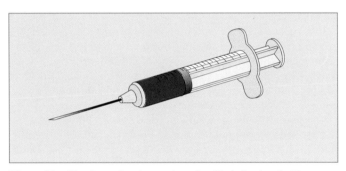

When taking blood samples, do not clean the skin beforehand with methylated spirits

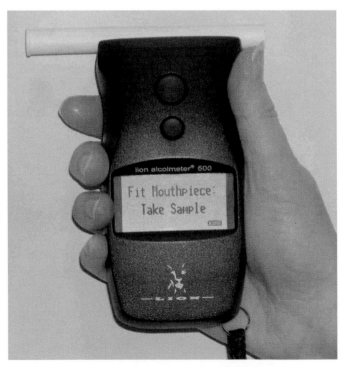

Breath alcohol concentrations accurately reflect the blood alcohol concentration, are simple to test with an alcolmeter, and provide an immediate result

Barry, Wales) costs around £600; additional costs relating to tubes for blowing into and regular maintenance are involved. Alcolmeters have been used successfully in hospitals and general practice, but if the reason for their use is not explained carefully, patients may perceive them as a threat.

Urine

Levels of alcohol in urine also can be measured: a value that exceeds 120 mg/100 ml (26 mmol/l) is suggestive of alcohol misuse and a value higher than 200 mg/100 ml (43.4 mmol/l) is diagnostic. Samples should be kept in a refrigerator (preferably frozen) until analysis, otherwise false positive results will be obtained, especially in patients with diabetes, because of fermentation of glucose.

The "Cage" questions are reproduced from Mayfield D et al. *Am J Psychiatry* 1974;131:1121-3. The chart showing the laboratory markers of alcohol misuse is adapted from Chick J et al. *Lancet* 1981;i:249-51 (γ glutamyl transferase and mean corpuscular volume) and Whitfield JB et al. *Ann Clin Biochem* 1978;15:297-302 (urate). The photograph of the alcolmeter is with permission of Lion Laboratories Ltd, Barry, Wales. The AUDIT questionnaire was developed by the World Health Organization.

Further reading

- Berger A. Alcohol breath testing. *BMJ* 2002;325:1403
- Saunders JB, Aasland OG, Babor TF, de la Fuente JR, Grant M. Development of the Alcohol Use Disorders Identification Test (AUDIT): WHO collaborative project on early detection of persons with harmful alcohol consumption—II. *Addiction* 1993;88:349-82
- Selzer ML, Vinokur A, van Rooijen L. A self-administered Short Michigan Alcoholism Screening Test (SMAST). *J Stud Alc* 1975;36:117-26
- Sharpe PC, McBride R, Archbold GPR. Biochemical markers of alcohol abuse. *Q J Med* 1996;89:137-44
- Stockwell T, Hodgson R, Edwards G, Taylor C, Rankin H. The development of a questionnaire to measure severity of alcohol dependence. *Br J Addict* 1979;74:79-87

7 Problems in accident and emergency departments

Robin Touquet

Accident and emergency departments are a place of safety. Every year in England and Wales, 14.3 million patients attend accident and emergency departments unexpectedly—in trouble and needing help and professionalism. Nearly one third (30%) of attendances are related to alcohol and cost £0.5 billion a year; however, between midnight and 5 am, the number of attendances related to alcohol increases to 70%. The total cost to the NHS for all harms related to alcohol is £1.7 billion, and the cost for alcohol related crime, excluding drink driving, is another £1.8 billion.

Patient with Colles' fracture holding his own bottle of "thunderbird"

Role of accident and emergency department

Attendance at accident and emergency departments as a result of alcohol misuse is a "teachable moment"—when the patient can decide to moderate their drinking. Brief intervention (Chapter 13) serves to reinforce this: the sooner in the patient's drinking life it is carried out, the greater its effectiveness.

Motivation to reduce alcohol intake is greater if the person is able to make the link between excessive consumption and harm to their health; such a link may be particularly clear during a visit to an accident and emergency department. Several important barriers to detection (screening) and intervention exist, however: clinical inertia, limited time for managing patients (particularly important), and staff's negative attitudes to opportunistic identification of alcohol misuse. Accident and emergency departments are busy environments with high patient turnover, and national requirements to reduce waiting times have added to the pressure to treat people as quickly and efficiently as possible. Identifying and managing alcohol misuse therefore is a challenging task.

People who misuse alcohol may attend accident and emergency departments for conditions directly related to their drinking. In some cases, the alcohol problem can be recognised by the person's appearance or behaviour or with the use of a questionnaire. It is important to remember that the patient may have sobered up by the time they reach hospital, so other clues will be needed to arouse suspicion (see Chapter 6). In addition, alcohol misuse is responsible for a great many social problems, and you should bear in mind that the person who attends may be the victim rather than the misuser of alcohol, especially in the case of injuries from violence, marital disputes, "granny bashing," non-accidental injury in children, and accidents.

"Top 10" conditions associated with alcohol that present in accident and emergency departments

- Fall
- Collapse
- Head injury
- Assault
- Accident
- Feeling unwell
- Non-specific gastrointestinal symptoms
- Psychiatric symptoms
- Cardiac symptoms
- Repeat attendance

Detection

Questionnaires are a useful means of detecting people who misuse alcohol, and the Paddington Alcohol Test has been designed for this purpose, as a brief, pragmatic, clinical tool for use when time is at a premium (see Chapter 6). It lists the "top 10" conditions that present in accident and emergency departments and have the highest association with alcohol misuse as an aide memoire. These conditions cover approximately 60% of all attendances and reap the most fruitful harvest of drinkers for the time spent applying the questionnaire, especially through the question, "Do you feel your current attendance is related to alcohol?" Selective, focused screening reveals a crop of patients who have the greatest chance of a positive response and lowest likelihood of

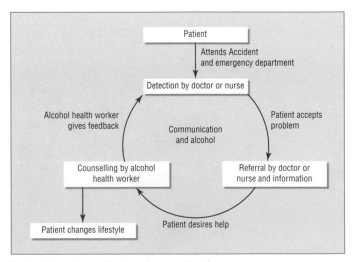

Cycle of detection, referral, and counselling

reattending if they can be made to understand cause and effect—the link between their drinking and their attendance at the accident and emergency department.

Screening is accompanied by the offer of referral to a dedicated alcohol health worker for those who misuse alcohol. Attendance at an appointment is more likely with increasing age and in patients who complained of feeling ill when first seen. The benefits of this approach were shown in a randomised trial that found that for every two referrals to the alcohol health worker, one less reattendance occurred during the next 12 months. If patients are offered an appointment with the alcohol health worker on the same day, almost two thirds attend; when the gap is two days, the number who attend drops to 28%. The half life of the "teachable moment" thus is less than 48 hours.

Education and training

Staff's understanding of the various presentations of alcohol misuse in accident and emergency departments usually is limited, as is their perception of what can be done for people who misuse alcohol (the same problem arises throughout the NHS). This can be remedied by giving people likely to come in contact with patients with alcohol problems induction training that emphasises the value of identifying hazardous drinkers early on in their drinking life—before the risk of dependency— and the value of brief intervention. Such training should be followed by regular audit of numbers detected and numbers referred to the alcohol health worker. The patient's general practitioner needs to be informed, as they may be unaware of the patient's misuse of alcohol.

Junior medical staff and others who work in the frenetic and challenging environment of the accident and emergency department look for encouragement and support from senior staff. Education, feedback, and audit result in detection of at least 50% of patients with the top 10 conditions listed in the Paddington alcohol test. More senior staff—consultants, registrars, and nurse practitioners—may find it difficult to adapt to these procedures as selective, focused screening may well be new to them. Their often negative, preconceived views can be entrenched, and the drinking habits of doctors and nurses, combined with their own cultural attitudes, influence whether or not they will use the Paddington alcohol test.

A recent report from the Royal College of Physicians recommended that all acute hospitals use alcohol health workers to counsel those who misuse alcohol. Such workers should be available throughout the working week to maximise attendance at appointments and make best use of the "teachable moment." They also act as a focus for education, support, and feedback for other staff. In the environment of the accident and emergency department, it is all too easy for a junior doctor or nurse to forget to apply the Paddington alcohol test. **The practitioner should always attend to the patient's agenda first, thus ensuring cooperation, before introducing their own agenda of the test.**

Simple use of Paddington Alcohol Test (PAT) (see also Chapter 6)

1 Deal with the patient's presenting condition **first** to **gain their confidence**, so that they are in a more receptive frame of mind
2 If the patient has a top 10 condition, as listed on the Paddington alcohol test sheet, or another indication of recent consumption of alcohol, use question 1 to ask the patient if they drink: "We routinely ask all patients in the accident and emergency department if they drink alcohol—do you drink?"
   —If the patient does not drink, they are negative in this test and the test can be discontinued (as long as their doctor agrees)
   —If the patient does drink, use question 2 ("Quite a number of people have times when they drink more than usual; what is the most you will drink in any one day?") to find out how much they drink in one session. The amount of alcohol in different drinks varies substantially, so an estimate of units drunk is needed for consistency. To focus solely on quantity is less judgemental
3 Make a rough calculation of the number of units drunk
   —If the number of units drunk is more than the threshold of eight units for men or six units for women, ask question 3: "How often do you drink this amount?" This helps differentiate the dependent drinker, who will need more complex management, from the hazardous drinker
   —If the number of units is less than the threshold, ask question 4: "Do you feel your current attendance at this accident and emergency department is related to alcohol?"
4 If the patient has evidence of chronic alcohol misuse and confusion, ataxia, or ophthalmoplegia, give them intravenous Pabrinex I and Pabrinex II (X2) in 100 ml 0.9% saline infused over half an hour
5 All patients who answered yes to question 1 should be asked question 4. If the answer to question 4 is yes, this starts the process of brief intervention, in which the patient associates drinking with their resulting attendance at the accident and emergency department. If they deny any association, but in your clinical judgement had been drinking, say: "If you had **not** been drinking you would not be in the department now!"

The earlier binge drinking is detected, the more effective is the use of the Paddington alcohol test, which itself is the start of brief intervention. Patients' acceptance of an appointment with an alcohol health worker shows awareness of a problem and the desire for help, thereby showing insight.

Brief intervention by alcohol health workers—or the relevant follow up service in your own department (which may be from the local mental health trust)—provides a booster to the Paddington alcohol test, with further likelihood of decreased consumption.

Every two referrals to alcohol health worker means one less reattendance during the next year

ALCOHOL – can the NHS afford it?
RECOMMENDATIONS FOR A COHERENT ALCOHOL STRATEGY FOR HOSPITALS

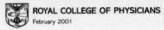

ROYAL COLLEGE OF PHYSICIANS
February 2001

The report recommended that all acute hospitals should employ health workers to counsel those who are misusing alcohol

Detection and counselling

Two stage process
1. Practitioner detects
2. Alcohol health worker counsels
How to conquer "clinical inertia"—pay off for practitioner is reduced reattendance

Resuscitation

All too often, the underlying cause of a collapse is misuse of alcohol. Although the usual coordinated approach enshrined in airway, breathing, and circulation (ABC) should be followed, causes of collapse need to be considered. In the case of alcohol misuse, this may cross different specialties—for example, patients who have drunk and overdosed on multiple substances (general medicine and psychiatry) and jumped from a height (surgery). Children who drink "alcopops," bottles of cider (cheaper), or even "adult" drinks are a particular concern, as they are at risk of hypoglycaemia, as well as the complications that are associated with drunkenness.

Drunk people with head injuries always are difficult to manage, because a reduced score on the Glasgow coma scale may not be the sole result of alcohol misuse but perhaps the result of an intracranial bleed (subdural haematoma). Such patients, if dependent on alcohol, may have prolonged clotting times and a widened subdural space from cerebral atrophy. The axiom "gas them and scan them" is appropriate—that is, request an anaesthetist to ensure that the patient is motionless within the computed tomography scanner. Relatives who reject the patient in life may litigate in death to exorcise their guilt if the patient is mismanaged in the accident and emergency department.

Dependent drinkers

Dependent drinkers drink to excess—at least double the sensible levels (more then eight units for a man or six units for a woman) every day. If unable to drink, they crave alcohol and are liable to develop delirium tremens (DTs) that require specific medical treatment (see Chapter 13). Such people may still hold down their job and marriage, but their health will almost certainly deteriorate. At the extreme, people who drink heavily may have lost their job, their marriage, their home, and finally their dignity and self-respect, as they become "of no fixed abode." Such people, especially if unkempt, drunk, or abusive, may be unpopular with staff, but they need to be managed appropriately in the accident and emergency department in order to maintain their independence, even though they discharge themselves as soon as they have been treated. To try and reduce their dependence, they always should be offered support through referral to a dedicated alcohol health worker, a voluntary alcohol agency, or Alcoholics Anonymous.

Dependent drinkers risk developing Wernicke's encephalopathy from a combination of chronic alcohol misuse and poor diet. This is the result of thiamine deficiency and is relatively common and potentially lethal but reversible if treated early. The common signs of confusion, ataxia, and varying levels of impaired consciousness are difficult or impossible to differentiate from drunkenness, and the characteristic eye signs of nystagmus and ophthalmoplegia are present in only 25% of patients. If in doubt, therefore, parenteral B complex vitamins should be given while the patient is still drunk. Oral treatment is ineffective even if such patients are compliant. The only available intravenous treatment that includes thiamine (vitamin B_1), riboflavin (vitamin B_2), pyridoxine (vitamin B_6) and nicotinamide is Pabrinex (Parentrovite was discontinued in 1993). Two pairs of vials of Pabrinex 1 and Pabrinex 2 diluted in 100 ml crystalloid solution should be given intravenously over 30 minutes (anaphylaxis is rare). Intramuscular Pabrinex includes benzyl alcohol as a local anaesthetic and can be used in patients who lack venous access.

Hypoglycaemia also may be a feature of dependent drinking. It should be treated with intravenous glucose, and

Collapse because of alcohol

Type	System	Effect
Primary	Alcohol is a direct sedative	Unconsciousness
	Respiratory arrest	Death
Secondary		
Medical	Respiratory	Inhalation of vomit (especially the young)
	Cardiovascular system	Arrhythmia
	Central nervous system	Fits ("DTs")
	Gastrointestinal	Oesophageal varices from cirrhosis
	Pancreatitis	
	Blood clotting	
	Metabolic	Hypoglycaemia
	Endocrine	Diabetes
Surgical	Trauma	Accidents, especially head injury Personal violence
Psychiatric	Self-neglect Self abuse Interaction with legal (prescribed) or illicit drugs	No fixed abode Overdose or trauma

Dependent drinkers may be unpleasant

Signs
- Craving for alcohol
- Drinks to excess most days
- Signs of chronic alcohol misuse
- Repeat attender at accident and emergency departments
- Need to prevent Wernicke's encephalopathy

Management
- Paddington alcohol test
- Pabrinex
    —Intravenous infusion over 30 minutes
    —Risk of anaphylactic reaction is rare

Further reading
- Cabinet Office Strategy Unit. *Alcohol harm reduction strategy for England*, March 2004, www.strategy.gov.uk
- Cabinet Office Strategy Unit. *Alcohol misuse: how much does it cost?* London: Cabinet Office Strategy Unit, 2003
- Crawford MJ, Patten R, Touquet R, et al. Screening and referral for brief intervention of alcohol misusing patients in an accident and emergency department: a pragmatic, randomised, controlled trial. *Lancet* 2004;364:1334-9
- Huntley JS, Blain C, Hood S, Touquet R. Improving detection of alcohol misuse in patients presenting to an A&E department. *Emerg Med J* 2001;18: 99-104
- Touquet R, Fothergill J, Henry JA, Harris NH. Accident and emergency medicine. In: Powers MJ, Harris NH, eds. *Clinical negligence*. London: Butterworth, 2000
- Royal College of Physicians. *Alcohol—can the NHS afford it? Recommendations for a coherent alcohol strategy for hospitals.* London: Royal College of Physicians, 2001 (www.rcplondon.ac.uk)
- Thomson AL, Cook CCH, Touquet R, Henry JA. The Royal College of Physicians report on alcohol: guidelines for managing Wernicke's encephalopathy in the accident and emergency department. *Alcohol Alcohol* 2002;37:513-21

intravenous Pabrinex should be given to avoid Wernicke's encephalopathy being precipitated as the body's remaining thiamine is used up.

Conclusion

All staff should be aware of the ubiquitous nature of alcohol misuse, so they can grasp the opportunity to reverse the damage at a time when the patient is likely to heed advice and benefit from it. Numerous points of hospital contact other than the accident and emergency department would benefit from such an approach, for example, medical wards, fracture clinics, orthopaedic units, maxillofacial units, and sexually transmitted disease clinics.

The lesson to be learnt is that people who misuse alcohol need support as soon as possible after being recognised— any delay and they may be lost

8 Medical problems

Alex Paton

Before medical problems are discussed, it is worth emphasising that **more than 80% of the harm done by heavy drinking is socioeconomic rather than physical and that severe physical damage is uncommon and often irreversible**. Alcohol misuse is as common as diabetes, and it has replaced syphilis as the great mimic of disease. Its protean symptoms are compounded by the reluctance of drinkers, relatives, and health professionals to face up to there being a problem. In addition, as most organs in the body can be affected, the medical approach is that of the doctor looking for signs of gross disease. To concentrate on these is unhelpful and deceptive, because their absence gives a false sense of security. They will not be discussed in detail here; instead, we need to highlight the many non-specific symptoms, which are often vague, multiple, and psychosomatic and do not always fit into a recognisable diagnostic pattern.

A few heavy drinkers are referred to doctors because of their drinking and a few are picked up at health checks because of an enlarged liver or abnormal blood test, but most problem drinkers are missed because a drinking history is not obtained or because the importance of symptoms is not appreciated. Surveys show that around 20% of patients in medical wards drink too much but most are unrecognised; similar findings almost certainly apply to other hospital departments and general practice.

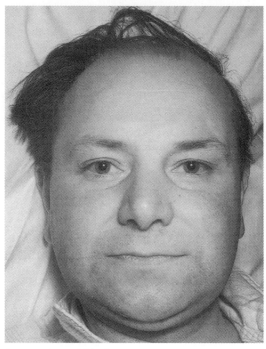
Spotting the problem drinker

Spotting the problem drinker

The brash, jocular, over familiar manner of the problem drinker, inappropriate to a consultation, may sometimes provide a clue, as might shifty answers to preliminary questions, as denial is common. Symptoms should be regarded sympathetically and not brushed aside, and it is important not to jump to conclusions and lose the person's confidence. Certain features in the history may provide other evidence. Sometimes the spouse is the person who attends because of problems with family and children, but they are likely to be reluctant to reveal the true cause.

Family history may reveal risk factors such as alcohol misuse, teetotalism, depression, a broken home, and being last in a large family. Drug taking, heavy cigarette smoking, marital disharmony, and drinking by the spouse may be features of a dysfunctional family.

People of Irish and Scottish descent seem to drink more than the English and to be more prone to physical damage. Other Europeans may have problems because they are socially accustomed to larger amounts of alcohol. The taboo against drinking among Muslim men is breaking down, and, as a result, they seem to be sensitive to damage but because of the stigma are reluctant to seek help.

Signs
If present, certain signs may be useful pointers: a bloated, plethoric face with telangiectases, bloodshot conjunctivae, acne rosacea, smell of stale alcohol (sometimes disguised by peppermint or aftershave lotion), and raw, red gums that bleed easily. About a third of problem drinkers have a facial appearance that resembles that of Cushing's syndrome.

The skin is warm and moist, with a fast bounding pulse and tremor of nicotine stained fingers, sometimes designated a pseudothyrotoxic state. Other signs to look for are palmar erythema, bilateral Dupuytren's contractures, parotid swelling

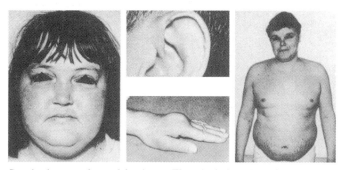
Certain signs may be useful pointers. These include a bloated, plethoric face (left), gouty tophi on hands and ears (middle), and obesity with a pot belly and gynaecomastia

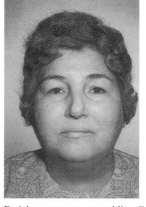 
Facial appearance resembling Cushing's syndrome is seen in about a third of problem drinkers. Before (left) and after (right) stopping drinking

(rare), and gouty tophi on ears or hands. Abdominal obesity is common and sometimes associated with gynaecomastia and abdominal striae. Bruising and scarring indicate old injuries.

Morbidity

Intoxication, for example from bingeing, can be associated with serious metabolic disturbance (alcoholic ketoacidosis), cardiac arrhythmias, nerve palsies, stroke, and respiratory failure.

The best known physical complication, used as a marker for alcohol damage, is cirrhosis of the liver, although fewer than 10% of heavy drinkers are affected. Numbers have been rising steadily, especially in women, which reflects the increase in misuse over the past 20 years. Other organs that are particularly sensitive have not been studied in such detail, but that constant exposure of the gastrointestinal tract to alcohol might lead to oesophagitis, gastritis, cancers of the mouth, oesophagus, and larynx (with heavy smoking), diarrhoea, and pancreatitis—one of the most unpleasant and painful consequences of misuse—is understandable.

Next in importance is the cardiovascular system, where hypertension and irregularities of cardiac rhythm are relatively frequent. Atrial fibrillation has been called "holiday heart" in the United States, because it occurs especially during weekend and holiday drinking among relatively naive drinkers. Ventricular arrhythmias are a likely cause of sudden death in intoxicated people. Alcohol can also precipitate heart muscle disease—cardiomyopathy—which used to be confined to men but is now being diagnosed increasingly in women.

Brain damage from alcohol misuse may be associated with strokes at a young age, cerebral atrophy, subdural haematoma, dementias, and Wernicke-Korsakoff syndrome, in which an acute confusional state can be improved dramatically by injection of thiamine (see Chapter 7); otherwise, progressive loss of memory for recent events occurs. Hallucinatory and amnesic states (blackouts and fugues), alcoholic psychosis, alcohol and drug overdose (often a lethal combination), depression, and suicide are well recognised.

Inadequate nutrition can result in beri beri from lack of thiamine, scurvy from deficiency of vitamin C, and macrocytic anaemia because of lack of folic acid. Heavy drinking depresses immunity, with a consequent risk of serious infections. Obesity, infertility, and poorly understood hormonal and metabolic changes may not always be recognised as the result of overindulgence.

Women in particular can suffer from menstrual disturbances and miscarriage, and if drinking is particularly heavy and continuous, fetal growth may be delayed and the child may subsequently suffer behavioural and cognitive impairment. Fortunately, the complete fetal alcohol syndrome is extremely rare, affecting babies of only 1% of mothers who drink really heavily. The usual advice given to women contemplating pregnancy in Britain is that they should avoid alcohol during conception and in the first trimester and be careful not to overconsume in the third trimester, when the brain is developing, but otherwise up to three units at a time is unlikely to be harmful. On no account should women feel guilty if they fail to stick rigidly to the guidelines.

Circumstances in which index of suspicion for heavy drinking should be high

- Repeated attendances or admissions for relatively minor complaints that cannot be labelled readily
- Gastrointestinal symptoms with no established cause
- Chest pain mimicking angina or palpitations due to arrhythmias
- "Essential" hypertension in men, which may not be adequately controlled by drugs
- Mild glycosuria in young or middle aged people
- Gout, whatever the immediate precipitating cause
- Attacks of confusion, especially in strange surroundings or after stress such as illness, operation, or bereavement
- Fits for the first time in middle age
- "Turns," falls, or incontinence in elderly people
- Unexplained anaemia or hepatomegaly
- Serious chest infections with poor response to treatment
- Endocrine features that mimic Cushing's syndrome, thyrotoxicosis, phaeochromocytoma, or carcinoid syndrome

"Come on in son, we'll soon get you into shape"

Obesity, infertility, and poorly understood hormonal and metabolic changes may not always be recognised as the result of overindulgence

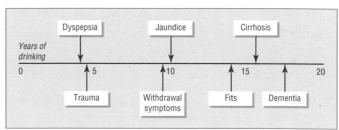

Pattern of complications during a heavy drinker's life

Conditions associated with heavy drinking

Gut and liver
- Morning anorexia
- Indigestion
- Heartburn
- Vomiting
- Bleeding
- Jaundice
- Oesophagitis
- Gastritis
- Mallory Weiss syndrome
- Aero-digestive cancers
- Diverticulitis
- Pancreatitis
- Hepatitis/cirrhosis/
  liver cancer

Gynaecological
- Irregular periods
- Premenstrual tension
- Infertility
- Miscarriage
- "Small for date" babies
- Fetal alcohol effects
- Fetal alcohol syndrome
- Breast cancer

Chest and heart
- Palpitations
- Chest pain; can mimic angina
- Bronchitis
- "Asthma"
- Arrhythmias
- Hypertension
- Lobar pneumonia
- Tuberculosis
- Fractured ribs
- Heart failure from beri beri

Hormones and metabolism
- Weight gain or weight loss
- "Sugar"
- Impotence
- Infertility
- Obesity
- Hyperglycaemia or
  hypoglycaemia (binge
  drinking)
- Pseudo-Cushing's syndrome
- Malnutrition—deficiencies of
  thiamine, vitamin C (scurvy),
  folic acid
- Alcoholic ketoacidosis (binge
  drinking)

Nervous system
- Tremor
- Sweating
- Flushing
- Insomnia
- Headache
- Blackouts
- Fits
- Confusion
- Inability to concentrate
- Problems with memory
- Anxiety or depression
- Hallucinations

Renal
- Loin pain
- "Blood in urine"
- Pelvi-ureteric obstruction
- Chronic nephritis
- Myoglobinuria from
  rhabdomyolysis

Skin, muscles, nerves and bones
- Bruises, scars
- Flushing
- Acne rosacea
- Psoriasis

- Weakness of thighs
- Myopathy
- Burning legs
- Peripheral neuropathy
- Saturday night palsy (binge
  drinking)
- Rhabdomyolysis (binge
  drinking)
- Dupuytren's contracture

- Backache
- Osteoporosis
- Rheumatism
- Gout
- Repeated injuries
- Fractures

Immune system
- Defective immunity
- Infections including AIDS

Mortality

Around 33 000 deaths a year in England and Wales are attributed to alcohol misuse. Lack of awareness among doctors and reluctance to include alcohol on death certificates mean that this figure is likely to be an underestimate; for example, the death rate from cirrhosis may be up to five times the official figure. Furthermore, numbers are weighted heavily towards men, although women increasingly are affected and are more vulnerable.

Deaths are customarily divided into those **specifically related** to alcohol, namely intoxication and binge drinking, fatal accidents and violence, suicide, and organ damage known to be alcohol related, and those **associated** with alcohol excess, such as certain cancers, coronary heart disease and stroke, and some neuropsychiatric conditions. Death rates for the former have doubled in the past 20 years in both sexes. Drinking in amounts that cause biochemical changes is associated with twice the mortality of the general population.

"That's the trouble with us alcoholics. We're a dying breed"

Around 33 000 deaths a year in England and Wales are attributed to alcohol misuse

All kinds of deaths related to alcohol tend to be premature, occurring most often between the ages of 40 and 60 years

Is moderate drinking good for the heart?

A great deal of interest has been aroused by epidemiological evidence that moderate drinking is associated with a reduction in deaths from coronary heart disease. If the relative risk for non-drinkers is taken as 1, the relative risk may be as low as 0.5 in people who drink moderately and then rise again to exceed 1 in those who drink heavily—the U shaped or J shaped curve. This so called "protective" effect can be produced by as little as 1-2 units of alcohol two or three times a week, and seems to be because of alcohol rather than any particular type of drink. A possible reason is that alcohol reduces clotting and increases protective lipoproteins, although those who champion red wine point to the presence of antioxidants that may help combat oxygen free radicals produced during breakdown of alcohol.

BEER DRINKERS TAKE HEART

"Three glasses of beer a day (30g alcohol) should reduce the risk of heart attack by 25%"
British Medical Journal

… and take the brewery's commendation with a pinch of salt

Much epidemiological evidence for a "protective" effect is based on studies of white, middle class, middle aged men, and alcohol is unlikely to be a universal panacea against coronary heart disease. Women and young drinkers, in whom heart disease is rare, are underrepresented, as are heavy drinkers who may be expected to die prematurely from alcohol related damage. The benefit seems to be in older men and post-menopausal women. Calls to drink large quantities of, say, red wine "to protect the heart" should be resisted firmly, because excessive consumption not only **causes** heart attacks but also damages other organs.

The two cartoons in this chapter are reproduced by permission of Pressdram Ltd, London. Copyright Pressdram Limited 2004.

> **To equate the number of lives that** might **be saved by alcohol against those killed is to miss the point that alcohol in excess is** always **potentially dangerous**

Further reading

- Edwards G, Peters TJ, eds. *Alcohol and alcohol problems.* Edinburgh: Churchill Livingstone, 1994
- Day C. Who gets alcoholic liver disease: nature or nurture? *J Roy Coll Phys* 2000;34:557-62
- Kemm J. Alcohol and breast cancer. *Alcoholism* 1998;17:1-2
- Royal College of Physicians. *A great and growing evil. The medical consequences of alcohol abuse.* London: Tavistock, 1987

9 Surgical problems

James Huntley, Robin Touquet

Alcohol misuse places a major avoidable burden on many NHS services, including surgical services, where its effects are complex and multifactorial. Alcohol has acute and chronic effects on the body and mind, which predispose to a number of surgical conditions. Alcohol also has important social effects—for example, as a result of disinhibition, decreased judgement, and increased risk taking. Misuse may cause problems through direct pathophysiological effects or indirect effects of trauma and social harm.

Acutely intoxicated and chronic misusers run different risks, but the effects of alcohol are pervasive and interrelated. Alcohol misuse is a risk factor for a variety of surgical conditions that fall into two groups: traumatic and non-traumatic. Although overlap exists—for example, compartment syndrome can occur in the presence or absence of trauma—this chapter considers the two groups separately. Non-traumatic conditions are listed according to specialty.

Trauma

Trauma is the greatest cause of death in people aged <40 years. Drinking alcohol is a risk factor for violent behaviour, being a victim of assault, and increasing severity of injury in certain situations (for example, cycling accidents). Alcohol is a major factor in trauma of all types: accidental and non-accidental (for example, suicide attempts and parasuicidal behaviour), self-harm, and accidental and deliberate (assault) harm of others. It remains a major factor in road traffic crashes, although the intoxicated person is not always the driver: a sober driver may strike a drunk pedestrian.

Trauma related to alcohol is common to all surgical specialties, especially general, orthopaedic, plastic, neurosurgical, maxillofacial, and ear, nose, and throat surgery. The pattern has changed in recent decades, with fewer "accidents," presumably because of public education, legislation, and practical enforcements (such as traffic calming measures), but an increase in injuries related to alcohol because of violence—this is a particular feature of alcohol misuse in the United Kingdom. Ninety per cent of victims of assault sustain single or multiple lacerations, bruises, or contusions, and only 10% a fracture. Acutely intoxicated people are vulnerable targets—"easy meat in the urban jungle."

Head injuries also are common. Of the one million patients who attend accident and emergency departments with a head injury each year (8% requiring admission), approximately 25% have drunk alcohol. This group presents a considerable management dilemma in terms of assessment, because the signs of intoxication and severity of head injury easily may be confused.

Non-trauma

The pervasive effects of alcohol misuse—defined as 64 g (eight units) for a man or more of ethanol a day for several months—may be classified into three phases:
- **Preoperative**—Alcohol is a risk factor for a number of conditions managed by surgical specialties
- **Perioperative**—Intraoperative problems include those of alcohol related comorbidity, such as cardiac dysfunction, altered hepatic metabolism of anaesthetic agents, prolonged clotting, and altered tissue quality

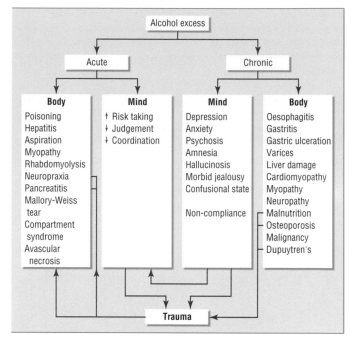

A web of causality

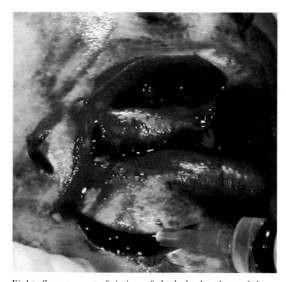

Eighty-five per cent of victims of alcohol related assault have a facial injury and 57% of individual injuries are to the face: lacerations right side of mouth

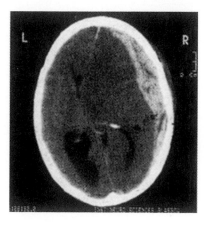

Right sided subdural haematoma with midline shift and left ventricular dilatation

- **Postoperative**—Increased risk of complications because of decreased immune function, poor wound healing, and non-compliance.

Intraoperative and postoperative effects may be important in surgery for conditions ostensibly unrelated to alcohol misuse (for example, total knee replacement). Dependent drinkers are at high risk of developing alcohol withdrawal syndrome in the postoperative phase, which classically manifests as an acute confusional state.

Preoperative problems

Gastroenterology

Upper gastrointestinal bleeding—Although surgery is effective in many forms of upper gastrointestinal bleeding, it carries high morbidity and mortality, especially in people who misuse alcohol. It generally is reserved for people in whom endoscopic treatment has failed.

Pancreatitis—Pancreatitis is an inflammatory condition in which the endogenous enzymes are activated and digest the pancreatic parenchyma—the most common causes are gallstones and alcohol. The pathogenesis is not completely understood, and the severity of the condition ranges from mild and self-limiting to extremely toxic, with a profound systemic inflammatory response that can lead to multiorgan failure and death. When **acute**, onset is usually 12-48 hours after an episode of binge drinking and is associated with nausea, vomiting, and high levels of amylase in plasma. In **chronic** pancreatitis, long term morphological damage occurs to the pancreas, with possible exocrine and endocrine deficiencies. The pain is chronic and can be extremely severe, in spite of which the person continues to drink.

Liver cirrhosis—Liver cirrhosis is increasing in incidence in the developing world, especially in young women, is usually secondary to alcohol misuse, and is a common cause of premature death in adults aged 25-64 years. The diagnosis carries a bleak prognosis and is expensive in terms of operative intervention—for example, management of portal hypertension, upper gastrointestinal bleeding, and liver transplantation. Worldwide, alcoholic cirrhosis is the second most common indication for liver transplantation, but patients need careful selection and a period of successful preoperative abstinence. Survival rates at one and five years after liver transplant are broadly similar for patients with alcoholic cirrhosis and other types of cirrhosis.

Orthopaedic surgery

Osteoporosis—Alcohol is held responsible as a major aetiological factor for osteoporosis, especially in men, but the evidence is equivocal. In vitro experiments show that alcohol is toxic to osteoblasts, but the situation seems to be different in vivo. Several epidemiological studies suggest that patients who abuse alcohol chronically have low bone mineral density and a high risk of fracture. Moderate alcohol use may be beneficial, however, and the confounding roles of nutritional deficiencies and smoking have not been elucidated.

Neuropathy, neuropraxia, and myopathy—These conditions do not need any surgical treatment, but patients with them frequently present to surgeons. Chronic alcohol misusers may develop bilateral, sensorimotor, symmetrical **neuropathy**, especially of the legs; this commonly is related to thiamine deficiency. Nerve compression (**neuropraxia**)—for example, of the radial nerve in the axilla and mid-humeral level—causes segmental demyelination, with loss of sensation and muscle power. Recovery generally occurs over days to weeks, and the only measure needed is appropriate soft splintage, such as a lively splint to keep the hand in position of function.

Non- traumatic surgical conditions	
Abdominal	• Upper gastrointestinal bleeding • Pancreatitis—acute and chronic • Liver cirrhosis • Portal hypertension
Malignancy	• Oesophageal cancer • Breast cancer • Colorectal cancer • Hepatocellular cancer
Orthopaedic	• Osteoporosis • Neuropraxia • Myopathy • Neuropathy • Avascular necrosis of femoral head • Rhabdomyolysis • Dupuytren's contracture
Neurosurgery	• Intracranial haemorrhage
Maxillofacial and ear, nose, and throat	• Nose bleeds • Myopathy • Carcinoma of larynx
Obstetrics	• Fetal alcohol syndrome • Fetal alcohol effects

Alcohol related causes of upper gastrointestinal bleed

- Peptic ulcer (increased incidence in portal hypertension)
- Varices
- Alcoholic haemorrhagic gastritis
- Portal gastropathy
- Mallory Weiss tear (oesophageal tear)
- Boerhaave's syndrome (ruptured oesophagus)
- Gastric carcinoma

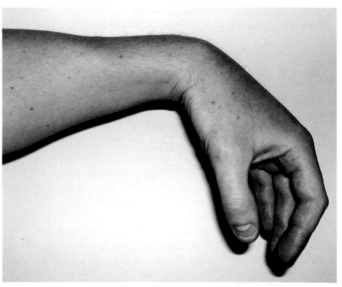

Radial nerve "Saturday night" palsy—drunken sleep with arm over back of chair

Alcohol misuse causes acute and chronic forms of **myopathy**. Muscle pain—especially around the hip, shoulder girdle, and thighs—with muscle swelling and proximal muscle weakness follow a period of acute intoxication. Severity varies, but typically the condition is mild, self-limiting, and resolves fully with a period of abstinence. A more serious form is rhabdomyolysis, myoglobinuria, acute tubular necrosis, and renal failure (see below).

Compartment syndrome—This is a condition in which the intracompartmental pressure rises to such a degree, relative to diastolic blood pressure, that perfusion to intracompartmental structures is compromised, leading to hypoxia and tissue death. Young athletic men are at particular risk. It is characterised by severe pain (especially on passive stretch of tendons passing through the compartment) and pain greater in severity than expected from the injury sustained. In addition, paraesthesiae, paralysis, pallor, and coolness occur. The presence of a distal pulse is not reassuring; indeed, this is normal in compartment syndrome. People who misuse alcohol are at high risk of this important condition. If the diagnosis is a possibility, compartment pressure monitoring should be the norm, as it expedites emergency and limb saving fasciotomies.

Rhabdomyolysis—This condition, fortunately rare, is characterised by damage to sarcolemmal membranes of skeletal muscle, which allows leakage of myoglobin and other intracellular contents (including creatine kinase and potassium ions) into the systemic circulation. A variety of triggers exist, but the two most common are mechanical injury (because of local compression and crushing) and alcohol misuse. Alcohol related rhabdomyolysis may be because of a mechanical effect (trauma or seizures) or a direct toxic effect on the membrane. Myoglobin is nephrotoxic and can precipitate acute tubular necrosis and renal failure. Hyperkalaemia, which may lead to cardiac arrest, occurs because of the leakage of potassium ions from the muscle, nephrotoxic effects, and renal failure.

Avascular necrosis of the femoral head—Non-traumatic osteonecrosis of the **femoral head** in the mature skeleton, most often bilateral, occurs mainly in men aged 35-45 years. A high index of suspicion should be maintained for patients with hip pain (especially at night), the severity of which is out of proportion to the clinical and radiological findings. The aetiology is multifactorial, with 40% of cases being idiopathic.

Dupuytren's contracture—This condition involves fibrosis and contracture of the palmar fascia, typically in men of Scandinavian descent, and is usually bilateral. Case-control studies suggest that alcohol is an independent risk factor for this condition, but smoking seems to be more important.

Neurosurgery
People who misuse alcohol are at high risk of intracranial, especially subdural, haematomas. Chronic misusers may not only have coagulopathy but also a degree of cortical atrophy, which renders the bridging veins more susceptible to damage.

Obstetrics
Misuse of alcohol in pregnancy is associated with fetal alcohol syndrome. Although smaller amounts of alcohol may be associated with less severe manifestations (fetal alcohol effects), interventricular haemorrhage and white matter damage are more likely in fetuses of women who drink more than three units on a single occasion. Minimal social drinking, however, has not been shown to be associated with increased risk. Opinion is divided as to what constitutes the best advice for pregnant women: in the United States, complete abstinence is recommended, while in the United Kingdom, occasional drinking within sensible limits is considered safe (see Chapter 8).

> Chronic myopathy is progressive and painless, resulting in weakness and wasting of the proximal limb muscles. Abstinence may improve the situation, but residual damage is likely

---

High risk of compartment syndrome during episodes of acute intoxication
- The individual is more likely to sustain a crush injury to an extremity (for example, calf left over edge of table)
- The individual is more likely to be involved in a traumatic incident resulting in high energy fracture (for example, bumper injury causing tibia fracture)
- Chronic misusers of alcohol may have coagulopathy that allows extravascular haemorrhage

---

Precipitants of avascular necrosis of the femoral head
- Alcohol
- Corticosteroids
- Irradiation
- Sickle cell disease
- The "bends"
- Gaucher's disease

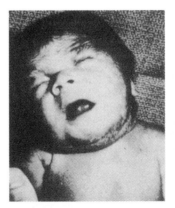 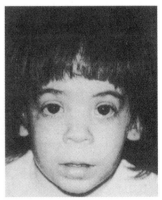

Infants born to mothers who drink may be damaged

Features of fetal alcohol syndrome
- Prenatal and postnatal growth retardation
- Behavioural disturbances
- Decreased intelligence quotient
- Heart abnormalities
- Facial abnormalities

Intraoperative problems

Misusers of alcohol may present a poorer surgical substrate—for example, they may have soft tissue and skin damage. In emergency situations, anaesthesia may be needed in an acutely intoxicated patient, but usually little recourse to history or indications of metabolic status is available.

A level of "basal narcosis" may mean that less general anaesthetic agent is needed to induce and maintain anaesthesia. In the context of chronic misuse, however, the central nervous system and metabolism of alcohol misusers undergo considerable alterations: clearance of some drugs—for example, propranolol, pentobarbital, amitriptyline, warfarin, and diazepam—may be enhanced dramatically by enzyme induction before cirrhosis develops. Induction involves up to a 10-fold increase in the microsomal ethanol oxidising system, with an associated increase in toxic aldehyde and oxygen free radical products, as well as conversion of certain xenobiotics (including paracetamol and anaesthetic drugs, such as enflurane and methoxyflurane) to toxic metabolites.

Once liver disease supervenes, drugs that are metabolised considerably by **first pass** mechanisms will have relatively diminished metabolism because of decreased hepatic blood flow, increased systemic shunting, and reduced hepatocellular function. The risk for these drugs is accorded on the basis of their physiological first pass metabolism. If synthetic function is compromised with hypoalbuminaemia, handling of protein bound drugs, such as corticosteroids, also is altered.

Postoperative complications

Although alcohol abuse and intoxication are associated with injury, accident, and assault, people who misuse alcohol are also at high risk of complications after surgery. For instance, case-match studies show that misusers with ankle fractures have significantly more in-hospital complications (33% vs 9%), longer hospital stays, more longer term complications, and greater requirements for further surgery. The increased risk is probably multifactorial. Similar effects have been documented for colorectal, upper gastrointestinal, prostate, subdural, and gynaecological surgery.

Stress response
Surgical trauma and alcohol activate the hypothalamo-pituitary-adrenal axis, and surgery increases activity of this more in long term misusers than normal drinkers. Indicators of surgical stress such as interleukin 6 are increased much less in heavy drinkers who have abstained for one month before surgery, and such a period of abstinence reduces postoperative morbidity considerably.

Wound healing
Alcohol misusers have a high risk of wound complications because of factors such as decreased immune function, altered haemostasis, nutritional deficiencies, and poor healing.

Bone healing
Myopathy, neuropathy, decreased osteoblast activity, nutritional deficiency, and poor compliance (concerning weightbearing, for example) all may contribute to delayed bone healing.

Haemostasis
Complications because of bleeding are a further problem. Alcohol has multiple effects on coagulation and fibrinolytic systems, which increase the bleeding time; this can manifest before, during, and after surgery. Chronic misuse of alcohol reduces the numbers of platelets and platelet aggregation in response to various stimuli. If the patient has liver disease,

---

Intraoperative problems for alcohol misusers

- Poor surgical substrate
- Basal narcosis
- Problems with drugs metabolised predominantly by first pass mechanisms
- Gastric distension, with the possibility of vomiting and aspiration, especially at induction
- Obtunding of autonomic responses: circulatory decompensation and shock may be precipitated with few warning signs
- Cardiac dysfunction because of cardiomyopathy with associated chamber dilation, valve annulus dilation (and hence regurgitation), and arrhythmias
- Hypoglycaemia from suppression of gluconeogenesis

Reasons for increased risk of postoperative complications in alcohol misusers

- Exaggerated stress response
- Changes in wound and bone healing
- Changes in haemostasis
- Changes in cardiovascular and hepatic physiology
- Changes in immune system
- Decreased self-care
- Non-compliance

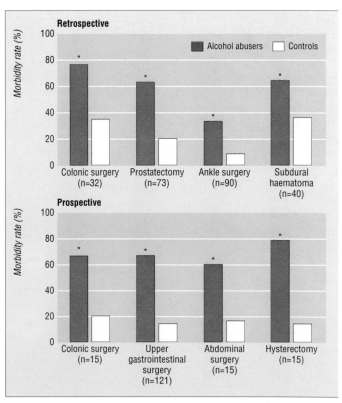

Retrospective and prospective studies of postoperative morbidity in people who misuse alcohol and controls

profound secondary coagulopathy may occur because of insufficient synthesis of coagulation factors.

Moderate drinking decreases levels of fibrinogen and increases fibrinolytic activity. This has been postulated as a possible mechanism for the proposed protective effect of alcohol against coronary heart disease.

Cardiovascular physiology
Alcohol misuse can cause myocardial damage and arrhythmia. One third of chronic drinkers are alleged to have a low ejection fraction because of cardiomyopathic changes. Subclinical defects may be unmasked only by the increased physiological demands from surgery.

Immune system
Chronic alcohol misuse is associated with an increased risk of infection and malignancy. Activation of T cells and T cell dependent processes are impaired; mobilisation of macrophages, mononuclear cells, and neutrophils is reduced; and delayed type hypersensitivity response is decreased.

Alcohol withdrawal syndrome
Alcohol withdrawal is a common cause of acute confusional states postoperatively and should be considered in all patients who present with features suggestive of this condition (see Chapter 13).

Conclusion

Clinical inertia is the failure of healthcare providers to offer, initiate, or intensify therapy when indicated. A large amount of identifiable alcohol misuse is undetected or undocumented. Furthermore, referrals to alcohol liaison services are offered infrequently. Problem drinkers often are seen as awkward nuisances rather than patients with identifiable problems and solutions. Patients who misuse alcohol rarely are optimised with a supported period of abstinence before elective surgery. Many opportunities for intervention when a patient has presented at a "moment of crisis"—and may therefore be amenable to change—are missed.

Early (that is, preoperative) recognition of people who misuse alcohol allows anticipation of possible complications and readiness to act on them. Furthermore, perioperative support can be optimised—for example, by a period of preoperative abstinence. Finally, the operative plan can be tailored towards the specific risks of the patient: for example, if the quality of the skin is poor, a different operative procedure might be indicated.

> People who misuse alcohol (drink more than eight units a day) have a threefold higher risk of postoperative morbidity than those who drink sensible amounts

---

> Considerable scope exists for organ function recovery after abstinence

---

> Abstinence for one month preoperatively considerably reduces postoperative morbidity

---

Further reading

- Boffetta P, Garfinkel L. Alcohol drinking and mortality among men enrolled in an American Cancer Society prospective study. *Epidemiology* 1990;1:342-8
- Elvy GA, Gillespie WJ. Problem drinking in orthopaedic patients. *J Bone Joint Surg Br* 1985;67B:478-81
- Shepherd J, Brickley M. The relationship between alcohol intoxication, stressors and injury in urban violence. *Br J Criminol* 1996;36:546-66
- Tome S, Lucey MR. Timing of liver transplantation in alcoholic cirrhosis. *J Hepatol* 2003;39:302-7
- Tonnesen H, Rosenberg J, Nielsen HJ, Rasmussen V, Hauge C, Pedersen IK, et al. Effect of preoperative abstinence on poor outcome in alcohol misusers: randomised controlled trial. *BMJ* 1999;318:1311-6
- Tonnesen H, Kehlet H. Preoperative alcoholism and postoperative morbidity. *Br J Surg* 1999;86:869-74

The photograph of the right sided subdural haematoma with midline shift and left ventricular dilatation is reproduced from the chapter on head injuries by Bullock R, et al. in Driscoll P, et al. (eds) *ABC of Major Trauma*, Oxford: Blackwells, 2000. The photograph showing fetal alcohol syndrome is reproduced from Clarren SK. *JAMA* 1981;245:2436-9. The charts showing retrospective and prospective studies of postoperative morbidity in people who misuse alcohol and controls are adapted from Tonnesen H, Kehlet H. *Br J Surg* 1999;86:869-74.

10   Drug-alcohol interactions

John Henry

Alcohol use is widespread, and almost everyone who consumes it will at some stage take prescribed or over the counter drugs; some will also take illicit drugs. This chapter provides a guide to how alcohol may interact with these substances, especially where there are potential adverse consequences.

Legal drugs

Sedative and hypnotic drugs

Alcohol increases the likelihood of intoxicant effects when taken with any drug that has a sedative effect on the central nervous system. This includes sedative and hypnotic drugs, such as benzodiazepines, opioids, tricyclic antidepressants, antipsychotics, and antihistamines (particularly older antihistamines). The effect may range from mild drowsiness to severe intoxication or coma, depending on the drug concerned and the amount of alcohol drunk. The main cautions involve

---

Sedative and hypnotic drugs combined with alcohol that increase likelihood of intoxicant effects
- Benzodiazepines
- Opioids
- Tricyclic antidepressants
- Antipsychotics
- Antihistamines (particularly older antihistamines)

Interactions between alcohol and prescribed or over the counter drugs

Drug group	Drugs involved	Possible effect
Angiotensin converting enzyme inhibitors	• All	• Enhanced hypotensive effect
Angiotensin II antagonists	• All	• Enhanced hypotensive effect
Analgesics	• Opioids	• Enhanced sedative effect
	• Non-steroidal anti-inflammatory drugs	• Enhanced gastrointestinal irritation
Antibacterials	• Metronidazole, cefamandole, cefoxitin, cefmetazole	• Disulfiram like interaction
	• Cycloserine	• Increased risk of seizures
	• Linezolid	• Reacts with tyramine in alcoholic and dealcoholised drinks, may cause hypertensive crisis
Anticoagulants	• Warfarin	• Enhanced anticoagulant effect with heavy regular consumption
Antidepressants	• Tricyclic and related	• Enhanced sedative effect
	• Non-selective monoamine oxidase inhibitors	• React with tyramine in alcoholic and dealcoholised drinks, may cause hypertensive crisis
	• Selective serotonin reuptake inhibitors	• Enhanced alcohol effects
Antidiabetics	• Oral	• Enhanced hypoglycaemic effect
	• Chlorpropamide	• Disulfiram like reaction
	• Metformin	• Increased risk of lactic acidosis
Antiepileptics	• Carbamazepine	• Central nervous system effects enhanced
	• Phenobarbital	• Reduced effect
	• Phenytoin	• Reduced effect
Antihistamines	• All	• Enhanced sedative effect
Antihypertensives	• All	• Enhanced hypotensive effect
	• Indoramin	• Enhanced sedative effect
Antimuscarinics	• Hyoscine	• Enhanced sedative effect
Antipsychotics	• All	• Enhanced sedative effect
Anxiolytics	• All	• Enhanced sedative effect
Barbiturates	• All	• Enhanced sedative effect
	• Phenobarbital	• Reduced effect
β Blockers	• All	• Enhanced hypotensive effect
Calcium antagonists	• All	• Enhanced hypotensive effect
	• Verapamil	• May increase blood alcohol
Cytotoxics	• Procarbazine	• Disulfiram like reaction
	• Disulfiram	• Disulfiram like reaction
Dopaminergics	• All	• Reduced tolerance to bromocriptine
	• Lofexidine	• Enhanced sedative effect
Muscle relaxants	• Baclofen	• Enhanced sedative effect
	• Methocarbamol	• Enhanced sedative effect
	• Tizanidine	• Enhanced sedative effect
	• Nabilone	• Enhanced sedative effect
Nitrates	• All	• Enhanced hypotensive effect
Paracetamol		• Hepatotoxicity possible
Paraldehyde		• Enhanced sedative effect
Retinoids	• Etretinate	• Acitretin formed from etretinate
Sedatives	• All	• Enhanced sedative effect

the adverse effects on driving and work skills because of the risk of accidents.

You should remember that this interaction applies not just to drugs given for their sedative effects but also to those that may produce sedation as a side effect. In some cases, the effect can be quite marked, particularly at the start of use, and patients should be reminded of this. Pharmacies add a warning on the label, which should reinforce any warnings given.

Warfarin

Many people take warfarin, the most widely used oral anticoagulant, and the question often arises as to how alcohol affects warfarin therapy. How much and how regularly can a patient safely drink alcohol without it interfering with the anticoagulant effect of warfarin? The answer is that small amounts of alcohol (≤2 units a day) are unlikely to interfere in the short or long term. Even a large single dose of alcohol is unlikely to affect clotting.

Regular consumption of ≥3 units a day increases warfarin metabolism because of induction of liver enzymes by alcohol, which results in a higher dose requirement for warfarin. As long as alcohol intake is kept stable, monitoring does not need to be increased. If alcohol intake changes considerably, however, close monitoring is needed. In a patient with late stages of alcoholic liver damage, production of vitamin K dependent clotting factors may be impaired, and warfarin will have a more marked effect.

Monoamine oxidase inhibitors

A number of drugs and foods that contain tyramine may interact with irreversible monoamine oxidase inhibitors (tranylcypromine and phenelzine) to produce a rapid and severe rise in blood pressure; the most likely symptom is a severe headache, but the main risk is of a cerebrovascular accident. Although alcohol itself does not interact with monoamine oxidase inhibitors, this warning also applies to many alcoholic drinks, especially some makes of red wine (typically Chianti), sherry, and some types of beer (including "alcohol free" beers), which have a high tyramine content.

Disulfiram reaction

Disulfiram (Antabuse) inhibits the liver enzyme aldehyde dehydrogenase, so that acetaldehyde accumulates and produces adverse effects when even a small amount of alcohol is drunk. This predictable and intended "disulfiram reaction" is why it is used as adjunctive therapy in alcohol dependence. Calcium carbimide and nitrefazole are also used for the same reason. Cardiac arrhythmias and hypotensive collapse may occur if large amounts of alcohol are taken. The effect can last up to 48 hours, or more, after the last dose of disulfiram.

The disulfiram reaction can also occur when several other drugs, typically metronidazole, furazolidone, and some second-generation cephalosporins (for example, cefamandole, cefoperazone, and cefoxitin), are taken with alcohol. Workers who have been exposed to dimethylformamide may also experience this reaction. Some types of edible mushroom can also cause it, particularly the ink cap (*Coprinus atramentarius*). A disulfiram like reaction also occurs with chlorpropamide and chloral hydrate.

Regular alcohol consumption

Most interactions described here refer to the "one off" interaction between alcohol and a drug. What about patients who drink alcohol regularly in considerable amounts? Regular, heavy use of alcohol has two main effects from the point of view of drug interactions: it induces liver enzymes, increasing the

> **Overdose of sedative and hypnotic drugs with alcohol can lead to severe central nervous system depression; the outcome can be fatal**

> **The risk of interaction between alcoholic drinks with high tyramine content and irreversible monoamine oxidase inhibitors continues up to two weeks after the drug is discontinued**

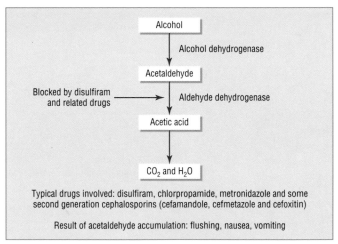

Typical drugs involved: disulfiram, chlorpropamide, metronidazole and some second generation cephalosporins (cefamandole, cefmetazole and cefoxitin)

Result of acetaldehyde accumulation: flushing, nausea, vomiting

Disulfiram reaction

Typical effects of disulfiram reaction
- Facial flushing
- Throbbing headache
- Shortness of breath
- Giddiness
- Palpitations
- Nausea and vomiting

breakdown rate of certain drugs (for example, phenytoin, with the risk of breakthrough seizures in patients on antiepileptic treatment), and it causes liver damage, reducing the liver's capacity to metabolise many drugs, with the risk of increased effects. This applies particularly to opioids and benzodiazepines, with the risk of toxicity from increased sedation.

Analgesics

Aspirin and the non-steroidal anti-inflammatory drugs have the potential to cause gastrointestinal bleeding because of their irritant effect and because they can prolong the prothrombin time. This is aggravated by alcohol consumption, as alcohol is also a gastrointestinal irritant, and in patients with severe alcoholic liver disease, blood clotting may be deranged. Patients should be warned about the possibility of this interaction, especially if they are taking prolonged courses of non-steroidal anti-inflammatory drugs. Gastrointestinal irritation because of these drugs may be worsened by concomitant alcohol intake.

Caffeine

Although caffeine has an undoubted stimulant effect, and popular lore suggests that strong black coffee is a good "antidote" for alcohol intoxication, no scientific evidence backs up the assumption that coffee aids the sobering up process. The only point in its favour is that the extra time taken to consume the coffee may allow the liver to metabolise more alcohol.

Illicit drugs

Heroin

Many heroin users also drink alcohol, and any central nervous system depressant (including alcohol and benzodiazepines) will increase the depressant effect of opioids such as heroin or methadone. The likelihood of fatal intoxication is higher in heroin users who have also drunk alcohol; this is an important issue to reinforce with patients who may misuse drugs.

Cocaine

Although alcohol is a depressant, cocaine is a stimulant. Their effects might be expected to cancel each other out, and although this does happen to some extent, alcohol taken at the same time as cocaine produces a new chemical: ethylcocaine or cocaethylene. Cocaethylene has similar effects to cocaine, but a considerably longer half-life, so that its effects are prolonged, and the "crash" after use of cocaine is diminished.

Amphetamine ("speed")

Amphetamine produces increased alertness and euphoria and impairs judgement. Although alcohol in small doses may reduce the effect of amphetamine, larger doses will almost certainly cause increased impairment. The use of amphetamine to reduce alcohol intoxication is not recommended.

Ecstasy (MDMA)

Alcohol and ecstasy interact by making the user feel more intoxicated. The "ecstasy" group of drugs, by releasing serotonin, produces a marked increase in antidiuretic hormone production. Because of this, large amounts of fluid taken together with ecstasy can lead to drowsiness, confusion, and convulsions from cerebral oedema because of fluid retention (ecstasy induced hyponatraemia). In theory, alcohol should diminish this risk, because it reduces the production of antidiuretic hormone.

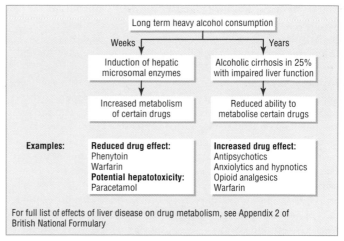

Long term alcohol consumption

Paracetamol, a widely used analgesic, is generally a very safe drug, except in overdose, when it may cause hepatotoxicity because of the consumption of glutathione, which leads to hepatocellular damage

Hepatoxicity in heavy alcohol drinkers when the therapeutic dose of paracetamol has not been exceeded, however, has been reported

Heavy users of cocaine who also consume alcohol know that the effects of cocaine last longer and are more economical

People who take ecstasy should replace fluid losses from dancing and sweating but should not consume excess fluid (alcoholic or non-alcoholic) if not exerting themselves

37

Gamma hydroxybutyrate (GHB; "liquid E" or "GBH")

This drug causes an alcohol like euphoria, and if taken regularly can lead to dependence and withdrawal. Its euphoriant and intoxicant effects will be aggravated by alcohol.

"Poppers"

Butyl and other nitrates (commonly known as poppers) are taken by club and partygoers for their brief, giddy, euphoriant effect and also for sexual enhancement. They can cause flushing, giddiness, tachycardia, and hypotension, and any hypotensive effect will be aggravated by alcohol consumption.

Cannabis

Cannabis considerably delays the absorption and reduces peak levels of alcohol. However, their effects on the mind are largely additive. Cannabis causes a sensation of relaxed intoxication, and alcohol taken at the same time is very likely to increase this effect, and it may also increase any sensation of confusion or disorientation. The combination of cannabis and alcohol markedly increases the risk of accidents caused by impaired judgement.

Poppers give a short lived euphoria but can also cause flushing, giddiness, tachycardia, and hypotension

Hepatitis C

Hepatitis C leads to the gradual development of hepatic cirrhosis over many years in about 25% of cases. Regular consumption of even small amounts of alcohol by people with hepatitis C infection, however, leads to more rapid development of severe liver disease than alcohol or hepatitis C alone.

Heavy drinkers should be tested for hepatitis C, and those who are positive for hepatitis C virus should be warned that any regular consumption of alcohol will markedly speed up the development of end stage liver disease and the need for a liver transplant

Further reading

- Hansten PD, Horn JR. Drug interactions, analysis and management. A clinical perspective and analysis of current developments. Germany: Wolters Kluwer Health Inc, 2004
- Hutchison TA, Shahan DR, eds. DRUGDEX system, Edition 119. Colorado: MICROMEDEX, 2004
- Stockley IH. Stockley's drug interactions, 6th edn. London: Pharmaceutical Press, 2002

The photograph of the poppers is reproduced from Tomlinson J (ed). *ABC of Sexual Health*, 2nd edn. Blackwell Publishing: Oxford, 2004.

11 Management of alcohol misuse in primary care

Geoffrey Smerdon

Alcohol misuse, like child abuse, usually is hidden. Drinkers are well aware of their problems and may bring them to the doctor, but many grow to rely on alcohol and cannot acknowledge, even to themselves, the connection between their problems and their drinking. The doctor therefore needs to be alert to the first clue, but, rather than taxing the patient with premature suspicions, it is better to gather more evidence. If alcohol is a significant factor, more than one clue is always present.

Detection

A number of screening tools have been devised for use in different settings and for different purposes (see Chapter 6). Questionnaires as a method of case finding in general practice have been found to require considerable resources, and the imposition of the doctor's agenda on patients who come for another purpose conflicts with the primary aim of making or keeping a healthy doctor-patient relationship. Receptionists involved in such programmes develop even more negative views, while subsequent compliance with follow up consultations shows a high attrition rate that is disappointing to patients and doctors.

Consumption

Self-reported consumption is an unreliable method for identifying alcohol misuse. Patients without problems may give accurate reports of their drinking, but only half of those with problems admit that they drink more than sensible limits when first questioned.

Clues

Clues are non-specific, and although no one clue is diagnostic, several should make the doctor increasingly confident that alcohol misuse is a significant factor. Confidentiality is not compromised by listening, although the general practitioner has a unique network of communications in the community from which to acquire a three dimensional view of the patient. Prolonged contact also means that the general practitioner can use repeated opportunities to gather information at a pace appropriate to the patient, who needs time to tell their story. Any sign that they are beginning to examine themselves should be encouraged, while gaps in the story should be noted and explored later. As always, diagnosis is incomplete without psychological, social, and physical assessment. Psychological and social clues of misuse develop long before physical signs. Signs of physical effects or damage often are sparse.

Investigations

No examination of a patient is complete without a review of the previous notes, including those of the family. The generally accepted view is that blood tests such as mean corpuscular volume and γ glutamyl transferase are of limited use, but, although they cannot diagnose alcohol misuse definitively, they can be used to enhance suspicion. Such conclusions are drawn from the pooled results of people tested. When individuals are considered, however, values of one or more markers closely mirror changes in alcohol intake. Experience in general practice confirms that these characteristics are constant over years, although some drinkers maintain normal values despite sustained alcohol misuse and resultant problems. Once a patient's personal pattern is established, therefore, blood tests, if

> Sensitive questioning of new patients, those having health checks or in risky occupations, and people with a clue, is the most acceptable way of identifying problem drinkers

> Use of a drinking diary (day, time, place, amount, and why) for a week is valuable, and drinkers often retrospectively increase their estimates—a measure of increasing honesty with themselves rather than with their doctor

---

Psychological and social clues of misuse

Primary clues	Secondary clues
• Evasion	• Being off sick
• Facile assurances	• Giving up interests
• Anxiety	• Out of character behaviour
• Unhappiness	• Problems at work
• Mood swings	• Debts
• Depression	• Conflict with others
• Sexual failure	• Changes of address or partner
• Other addictive drugs	• Neglect of children
• Suicide attempts	• "Lost" driving licence
	• Offences

Signs of physical effects or damage

- Smell of alcohol or peppermint on breath
- Previous injury
- Tender liver may indicate misuse
- Sweating and tremor may suggest withdrawal in a dependent drinker
- Organ damage is relatively late and uncommon, although it is as well to be aware that alcohol has the ability to affect almost every part of the body (see Chapter 8)

Typing of problem drinkers by blood tests

Type	Criteria	Prevalence of problem drinkers in a general practice (n = 122) (%)
M	• Mean corpuscular volume >95 • B-12 and folate normal • T4 and TSH normal	31
G	• γ glutamyl transferase >50 in men or >35 in women • Other liver function tests normal • No anticonvulsants or drugs	23
MG	• Meeting all criteria for M and G	33
O	• Mean corpuscular volume and γ glutamyl transferase normal • Serum ferritin >16 (serum ferritin <16 is a false negative)	13

M = mean corpuscular volume; G = γ glutamyl transferase; MG = both positive; O = neither positive

they show high levels, become a more reliable measure for monitoring relapses. They also become a valuable clue, because some patients have previous haematology or biochemistry reports in their notes, with abnormal results that were, at the time, overlooked.

Assessment of evidence

Once the available evidence has been checked, if alcohol use seems to be considerable, the doctor needs to share this opinion with the patient. Frankness administered by the doctor may be insufficient, therapeutic, or toxic: the dose is different for each patient. The doctor is unlikely to be the first person to suggest to the patient that they are drinking more than is good for them, and a frequent response will be well rehearsed: attempted diversion back to the problems and, if this is unsuccessful, anger and denial. Any sign of criticism will be seized upon by those seeking to defend their drinking. Patients will respond in one of two ways:

- They may continue to deny that they are drinking excessively or to admit it but claim that it is a reasonable response to their "real problems" or assert their right to continue nevertheless.
- They may accept that alcohol is damaging them and they need to change their drinking habits.

At any one time, only one in five of those with recognised alcohol problems in a general practice population are ready to change, but they have already taken the most important step towards recovery.

For those in the first group, attempts at persuasion tend to degenerate into argument. Progress depends on the patient's confidence in the doctor, and on the doctor's sensitivity as to when the patient is ready to accept some insight. The doctor can suggest that things are not likely to improve while the patient is drinking, offer further help if they change their mind, and maintain a watching brief. Patients with abnormal blood tests sometimes are keen to have these checked, which provides opportunities to maintain contact and use motivational interviewing to address internal conflicts that the patient is reluctant to acknowledge (see Chapter 13).

Many patients remain in the first group for years. Some eventually move into the second, influenced by family, friends, health professionals, events, crises, perhaps all of these, and—most often—"just getting fed up with the way I am." Others continue on a downward path, despite the best efforts of all involved, until they die prematurely. Hope, however, should never be abandoned, as a few will change even at the 11th hour.

Helping drinkers and families

Brief intervention

Brief intervention has been used for interventions that vary from 10 minutes of feedback, information, and advice to six hours of counselling. Drinkers who are ready to change, and who do not have symptoms of physical dependency or considerable psychological or social problems, may be able to do so with minimal help. The effective elements of such help are well summarised by the acronym FRAMES; this approach should be part of the repertoire of all clinical members of the primary care team.

Shared care

Consultations between general practitioners and drinkers often are mutually disappointing and frustrating. So much of a doctor's training is aimed at solving problems, and patients expect them to do this, but where lifestyle choices are the issue, a person centred approach is required. Doctor and patient need

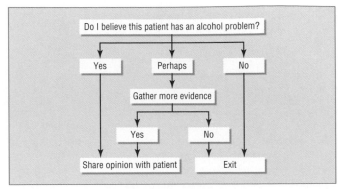

Do I believe my patient has an alcohol problem?

A case for motivational interviewing

"I lack willpower" she says, and you can't prescribe it.
Is willpower something you are born with in your genes and you are helpless? Or is this an excuse for a choice she has made, but doesn't like the consequences, so she dumps the blame elsewhere? Can you do anything constructive?

Yes
- Accept you cannot do it for her. If she wants it different she must find some way (her way, not yours) of making it so.
- Don't threaten her, she will only defend herself.
- She does what she does because she likes it. Find out what she gets out of it and appreciate it—she will feel understood.
- So where is the problem? Not your problem, hers. There must be some disadvantages to her choice; she knows this, but hasn't admitted it.
- Once she has looked at the good things and the bad consequences, does she want to change?
- If she does, you are in business. If she doesn't, at least she has made a choice. It is her own—you will both feel better for accepting it.
- She doesn't lack willpower, but she is not yet ready to move. It may take a crisis to shift her.

Frames*
- Feedback—Assessment and evaluation of the problem
- Responsibility—Emphasising that drinking is by choice
- Advice—Explicit advice on changing drinking behaviour
- Menu—Offering alternative goals and strategies
- Empathy—Role of therapist is important
- Self-efficacy—Installing optimism that chosen goals can be achieved

*Source: Miller WR, Sanchez VC. Motivating young adults for treatment and lifestyle change. In: Howard G (ed). *Issues in alcohol use and misuse by young adults*. Notre Dame, IN: Notre Dame Press, 1993

to make this shift. Many drinkers say they want to be cured of their addiction, but unfortunately no cure exists in the sense of an available and lasting remedy that can be applied to drinkers. They themselves have to take the responsibility for choosing and making necessary changes, and they deserve the credit when they succeed.

Drinkers may well try to engage the doctor (or counsellor if they are referred) into addressing their "real problems," but the first real problem to be addressed is the alcohol. Time is an important factor—not just time in therapy but time for the drinker to adjust. The condition has taken years to develop and seldom is overcome quickly. The ongoing relationship between general practitioner and patient allows a graduated response. If initial measures prove insufficient, more help can be arranged.

General practitioners seldom have the time or skills needed to function as the key worker for a drinker with established problems. This does not mean that general practitioners should refer these patients and switch off. If they have a good relationship, such abrogation is not appreciated, and if such a relationship does not exist, an opportunity to build one for the future is missed. The continued involvement of the general practitioner is needed to monitor the physical health of the patient, check blood tests, make arrangements for detoxification when required, and coordinate the help supplied to the patient's whole family.

Groups

In the maintenance phase of recovery, groups led by a key worker provide an economical source of help that encourages self-reliance. They are also useful for drinkers on a waiting list for one to one counselling. Patient groups run by Alcoholics Anonymous have a loyal following and a long record of success. Although they do not suit everyone, they are a valuable complement to the services available.

Key workers are to be found in various forms in different areas; they may be employed by the non-statutory agencies or the NHS. The quality of the shared care between general practitioner and key worker is a function of the communication between them. Each needs and can learn from the other to the benefit of their patients.

Families

Drinking may be a family activity, but even when only one member misuses alcohol, the others are caught up in the consequences. Psychological and social damage can be as severe for other family members as for the drinker, and physical damage in the form of violence is common. Public understanding of alcohol problems has improved in the past 20 years, but what remains as difficult as always is the journey that families have to make in acknowledging the situation, their own reaction to it, and how best to cope constructively.

Partners are also patients; they suffer and find it difficult to separate behaviour they hate from the person they love. They may be bitter, confused, and feeling guilty, but they often are willing to change their attitudes, and this may have a positive effect on the drinker. Help should be offered to partners of all established drinkers. Besides one to one counselling, patient groups can be very effective and are available from local agencies and from Al-Anon for partners, and Alateen for children.

Cutting down or stopping?

Many patients wish, initially, to deal with their drinking by cutting down. They underestimate the power of the addiction and the discipline needed for controlled drinking. Although a few may eventually succeed, most learn by experience that at

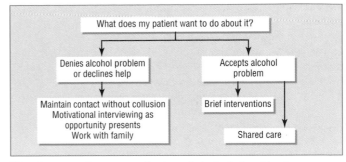

What does my patient want to do about their alcohol problem?

Conditions needed for key workers' best functioning

- Alcohol expertise
- Counselling skills
- Experience of carrying caseload in community
- Regular use of one to one clinical supervision
- Attachment to practices because take up by patients is higher there and shared care is easier

---

Action plan for individual drinker

Drinking too much (no complaints)
Advise
- Self help booklet
- Blood test
- Telephone number of local alcohol agency
- Help always available if required

Hazardous (risky) drinker
Help
- Brief intervention, up to three sessions
- Advise keeping a diary
- Involve key worker in practice or local alcohol agency
- Follow up if possible

Harmful (problem) drinker
Refer
- Home or hospital detoxification
- Refer to local alcohol agency, workplace programme if available, Alcoholics Anonymous or specialist unit
- Involve family

Dependent drinker
Refer
- Detoxification
- Refer to Alcoholics Anonymous, local alcohol agency, or specialist unit

---

least a considerable period of abstinence is needed. This is best achieved initially by supervised detoxification. Abrupt withdrawal often causes unpleasant symptoms; may result in serious complications such as status epilepticus, delirium tremens, or Wernicke-Korsakoff syndrome; and occasionally can prove fatal. For these reasons, detoxification needs medical supervision. Nevertheless, most detoxifications can be conducted safely at home by non-medical professionals, as long as an adequate protocol is followed and contraindications have been excluded (see Chapter 13). After detoxification, some drinkers try to persuade doctors to continue prescribing benzodiazepines as a way of helping them cut down or stop drinking; this should be avoided as it can lead to development of a second addiction.

Dual diagnosis

General practitioners who are accustomed to working with several diagnoses simultaneously should have no difficulty with the concept that alcohol misuse may be accompanied by another illness. While the patient is still drinking, and for some months after, they will do well to attribute psychological or psychotic symptoms and behaviour to the alcohol rather than to a mental condition, unless clear evidence of the latter existed before the drinking became serious.

Relapses and follow up

Relapses are part of normal recovery, and patients who resume drinking quickly revert to their previous pattern of behaviour. This may include a reluctance to admit what is happening, and questioning must be worked through again. Relapses, even after years, should not be seen as failure but as an educational opportunity to learn what factors precipitated the relapse and how these might be better dealt with in the future. The work that was done previously has not been wasted: patients who have relapsed move towards recovery more quickly than those doing so for the first time. When a patient is fearful of relapse, drug treatment may be considered (Chapter 13).

General practitioners, because of the list system, are well placed to follow up patients. An enquiry can be made when the patient attends for other reasons and a note made in the patient's record. Even when patients have moved, discreet questioning of other members of the family can establish whether recovered drinkers are still in control.

New general medical services contract

The specification for essential services under the new general medical services contract contains no mention of alcohol. A national enhanced specification for alcohol for general practitioners who want to offer additional care recommends a retainer of £1000 a year and a payment of £200 a quarter for each patient; these will increase by 3.2% annually. Although directed enhanced services must be provided in every area, national enhanced services are optional at the local level, so primary care trusts are free to make their own arrangements.

Conclusion

No experience is more instructive and rewarding than seeing an ingratiating, unreliable, duplicitous, and manipulative person become responsible, self-reliant, reconnected with others, and strengthened by their experience. Most of the care of drinkers and their families can be conducted in the community, as long as key workers are available in primary care. This enables specialists to concentrate on the patients who need their particular skills or facilities, which is the usual division of labour within the profession.

Minimum requirements for home detoxification

- Assessment—severity of alcohol dependence questionnaire (see Chapter 6) is useful for predicting withdrawal symptoms
- No major physical disease
- Drinkers to stay at home with 24 hour cover by a responsible adult or rota
- Drugs, titrated against symptom severity, using chlordiazepoxide for a week only
- Daily review by doctor or nurse

National enhanced service for alcohol misusers

- Up to date register of all who admit they are alcohol misusers. This will be used as an audit tool
- Practices able to undertake brief interventions
- Follow up treatment may be prescribed in conjunction with, or by referral to, local alcohol services
- Detoxification at home or in community may be provided when needed
- Routine use of assessment tools
- Liaison with local specialist alcohol treatment services
- Appropriate training must be available to primary care team members including detection, brief interventions, and follow up treatment including counselling
- Annual review, which could include an audit of those on the register, advice or treatment offered, number who have reduced alcohol consumption, and feedback from alcohol misusers and families

---

Further reading

- Bien TH, Miller WR, Tonigan JS. Brief interventions for alcohol problems; a review. *Addiction* 1993;88:315-36
- Bryant-Jefferies R. *Problem drinking—a person centred dialogue.* Oxford: Radcliffe, 2003
- Edwards AG, Rollnick S. Outcome studies of brief alcohol intervention in general practice—the problem of lost subjects. *Addiction* 1997;92:1699-704
- Morgan M, Colman J, Sherlock S. The use of a combination of peripheral markers for diagnosing alcoholism, and monitoring for continued abuse. *Br J Alc* 1981;16:167-77
- Sharpe P. Biochemical detection and monitoring of alcohol abuse and abstinence. *Ann Clin Biochem* 2001;38:652-64

12 Advice and counselling

Bruce Ritson

Alcohol use is a health issue, and people's drinking habits are, like smoking, a matter for clinical enquiry. Health professionals have a responsibility to take a drinking history, give clear advice about sensible drinking, and recognise alcohol related problems at an early stage.

Many people are sensitive about their drinking, and an offer of help will be more readily accepted if it is given in a spirit of concern for health and the family's wellbeing. To be judgemental usually is misplaced, and dire warnings are heeded rarely—unless they occur in a setting of mutual trust and respect. Once these preconditions exist, simple advice about changing habits often is surprisingly effective.

How to help and how to motivate

Most doctors are pessimistic about being able to help excessive drinkers, yet good evidence shows that **as many as two thirds respond well to treatment**. The family doctor and members of the primary healthcare team are particularly well placed to recognise the problem early and intervene.

Motivation is a rather suspect concept. We often blame drinkers for lack of motivation when relapse occurs, but, in common with many medical conditions, the treatment of alcohol problems is characterised by relapse and remission. Relapse is not necessarily the end of the therapeutic road, and the strength of motivation certainly is not constant. A reluctant patient brought by a desperate spouse or who attends to avoid dismissal from work often can be converted, with time, into taking responsibility for stopping or reducing their drinking.

The individual has acquired a drinking habit that is damaging their personality, family and social life, or health. It is wise to start by obtaining the patient's own views of their drinking. Argument and challenge rarely are helpful, and practitioners need to explain objectively the known facts relating to the individual's drinking.

Our habits are often hard to change, and people will be ambivalent about changing their drinking pattern. This often can be addressed directly by getting them to draw up a balance sheet of the good and bad consequences of continued drinking. Armed with such evidence, realistic goals for changing the drinking lifestyle should be negotiated. It is best to aim for specific short term goals at first, so the patient has a sense of achievement by attaining, for instance, three weeks' abstinence or even a party managed without disgrace, and then reporting progress. This is preferable to global but ill considered promises such as: "I will never touch another drop." Alcoholics Anonymous embodies the good sense of this approach in its recommendation that the misuser of alcohol should take "only one day at a time."

Changing lifestyle: impediments and alternatives

For many problem drinkers, drinking has become their predominant interest; to achieve the desired goal of reducing or stopping, they will in time have to make major changes to their way of life. Such people will need to confront impediments to change. These will either be evident from the initial balance sheet or will become clear as they try to change their habits. Examples include pressure from friends to continue drinking, a

Simple advice about sensible drinking and changing habits can be surprisingly effective

BALANCE SHEET		
Drinking	Advantages	Disadvantages
Continue	Forget my worries / Escape responsibility	Lose family / Health deteriorates / Cost
Reduce	Be like others / Appear "normal"	I found it hard and failed last time. Wife expects me to abstain and doesn't believe it possible
Stop	Please wife / Health improves / Save money	What to do with my time. What to tell my drinking friends

Filling in a balance sheet may help a patient realise the good and bad consequences of continued drinking

Triggers for drinking

- Habit
- Occupation
- Stress
- Interpersonal conflicts
- Depression and anxiety
- Withdrawal symptoms

job where drink is readily available, family stress with which the drinker cannot cope without a drink, an established neurosis or depression that has been masked by drinking, or the occurrence of withdrawal symptoms when trying to stop. The drinker should look out for situations, relationships, and feelings that "trigger" drinking and work out new ways of coping. A diary of drinking occasions often helps to identify such triggers.

At its simplest, people can be asked to think of activities they enjoy that do not involve drinking. The answer may initially be "none," but alternatives often become clearer if specific attention is paid to past triggers: for example, the drink at the end of the day can be avoided by going home earlier, the prematch drinks by meeting at the football ground, and so on. Anxiety may be relieved by relaxation training, but tranquillisers should not be used because of their potential for addiction. Sometimes more elaborate help focussed, for example, on tensions in the family may be necessary, but the doctor should never discount the more obvious, seemingly mechanical, and naive solutions that often prove surprisingly effective.

Elements of cognitive behavioural therapy are used widely to help people identify thoughts, feelings, and situations that trigger drinking behaviour. With the help of therapists, patients can develop and practice a set of psychological and social skills that help them counter triggers. Methods include coping skills for high risk situations and feelings, role modelling, and behavioural reversal.

Involve the spouse

The spouse is often the prime mover in seeking help. They should be involved actively in consultations, partly as an additional source of evidence about the true state of affairs, and as an aid to help the family find a new way of life that does not entail drinking. The family will have made certain protective adaptations to cope with its drinking members and will need to adjust to the new abstinent personality. Trust takes time to be re-established and the family will need support, particularly during periods of relapse when the spouse may believe that all is lost irretrievably. The spouse often feels confused, bitter, and devalued and will welcome the chance of being understood and participating in the process of recovery.

To drink or not to drink

If the patient's drinking is hazardous and hitherto harm free, health professionals should advise about sensible limits and clarify the guidelines. Risk of harm begins to increase as consumption rises above 21 units a week for men and 14 units a week for women. Current advice is for men and women not to drink more than four and three units, respectively, on any one occasion and to have two alcohol free days a week. Drinking should be kept to a minimum during pregnancy, and abstinence is the safest policy when driving or using other complex skills.

Some drinkers with established problems will return to moderate, harm free drinking, but it is difficult to predict who will succeed. Present evidence suggests that abstinence remains the safest goal for people aged >40 years, those who are seriously physically addicted, those who have signs of physical damage, and those who have tried controlled drinking without success. For younger people, whose problem drinking has been detected at an earlier stage and who are not seriously addicted or damaged, modified drinking may be acceptable and feasible. Most specialists have become less insistent on abstinence as the only goal, but controlled drinking needs to be carefully planned and discussed, and it is best preceded by a period of abstinence. It is wise to reach agreement with drinker and spouse over how to proceed.

If people can identify situations where they tend to drink, such as a drink after work, then they can avoid those triggers

Record exactly what you have drunk on each day last week

	Beers (pints)	Spirits (glasses)	Others including wine (glasses)	Place where consumed
Monday	3			Pub at lunchtime
Tuesday	4	2 whiskies		Pub / friends / evening
Wednesday				
Thursday	8			Evening / friends / payday
Friday	4 (lunchtime) 5 (evening)	2 whiskies		Row with wife
Saturday	2 (lunchtime)		1 bottle wine (dinner)	Home with wife
Sunday	2 (lunchtime)	2 whiskies (evening)		Pub with wife and friends

A drinking diary is a useful aid to self-audit

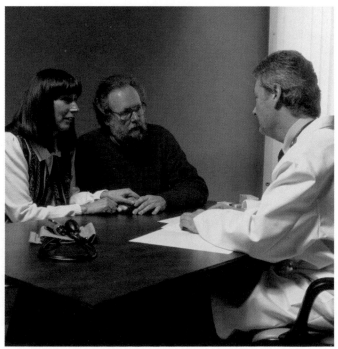

Where possible, the spouse should be involved in consultations

Review

Whatever the agreed goals, health workers must regularly review the drinker's progress. The most important tasks at the first interview are to gain their interest in tackling the problem and to try and ensure they will return for the next appointment, when short term gains can be applauded. Progress should be followed at intervals for at least a year; the first six months often give a good impression of longer term prognosis.

Laboratory tests—such as γ glutamyl transferase, mean corpuscular volume, and alcohol in breath—are useful objective means of monitoring progress, and the results and implications should be discussed with the drinker. A diary in which a note is kept of any drinks consumed, the time, the occasion, and the quantity is a useful aid to self-audit.

> **Relapse isn't the end of the road: set specific short term goals**

Relapse

Most people will drink again, whatever the original goal of treatment—often because of complacency and overconfidence that the problem is now in the past. This need not imply a catastrophic relapse involving the loss of all that has been achieved. It is more profitably viewed as an opportunity for the person to learn more about their nature and the problem itself. **Dealing with and learning from relapses is part of recovery.** It needs to be taken seriously by the professional and the drinker, and questions need to be honestly asked and answered. Once the anatomy of a relapse is laid bare, strategies for preventing recurrence will be recognised.

A closer study of relapses should help all parties identify the triggers, and it is helpful to list these. The family often feels particularly threatened and confused and will need extra support at this time. **Although setbacks may occur, therapeutic pessimism is misplaced, because the long term prognosis for problem drinkers is surprisingly good.**

The photograph of the doctor consulting with a patient is with permission of Antonia Reeve/Science Photo Library. The photograph of the people drinking in a pub after work is with permission of Ruth Jenkinson/Science Photo Library and the photograph of a couple consulting with a doctor is with permission of CC Studio/Science Photo Library.

Sources of advice

- National Drinkline (freephone 0800 917 8282) provides advice, information, and support to concerned people
- Alcohol Concern and Medical Council on Alcohol offer telephone advice, and a directory of voluntary alcohol agencies covering England and Wales is produced by the former. They provide free counselling to drinkers and their families, as well as education and training for alcohol workers and expert advice to other health professionals
- Alcoholics Anonymous and its associated family support groups can be contacted through their national helpline (0845 769 7555)

Addresses and telephones of these and other bodies are given at the end of Chapter 14, along with other information about self-help

Questions to address relapse

- What happened? A behavioural analysis
- When?
- Where?
- Who was there?
- How much did I drink?
- How often did I drink?

Further reading

- Dunn C, Devon L, Rivara FP. The use of brief intervention adapted for motivational interviewing across behavioural domains: a systematic review. *Addiction* 2001;96:1725-42
- Miller WR, Rollnick S. *Motivational interviewing. Preparing people for change.* New York: Guildford Press, 2002
- Morgan MY, Ritson EB. *Alcohol and health. A handbook for students and medical practitioners.* London: Medical Council on Alcohol, 2003:37-42
- Morganstern J, Longabaugh R. Cognitive behavioural treatment for alcohol dependence. *Addiction* 2000;95:1475-90
- Scottish Intercollegiate Guidelines Network. *The management of harmful drinking and alcohol dependence in primary care. SIGN guideline 74.* Edinburgh: Scottish Intercollegiate Guidelines Network, 2003. www.sign.ac.uk
- Wright N, Black N. Alcohol and primary care. Will an emphasis upon harm reduction engage general practitioners? *Br J Gen Pract* 2003;53:755-7

13 Treatments

Bruce Ritson

When hazardous or harmful drinking is first identified in primary care or the hospital setting, **brief intervention** should be offered. This consists of 10 minutes of discussion and explanation, provision of a self-help booklet, and the offer of a further appointment in one or two weeks. Its cost effectiveness has been proven, although time may have to be set aside rather than trying to undertake intervention within normal practice. Training and employing a member of staff for the purpose is worth consideration.

Motivational interviewing is of proven value. This essentially is an empathic, non-confrontational approach in which the doctor helps the patient identify their own reasons for change and strategies for achieving realistic goals. Essential components include sustaining commitment over time, involving the family where possible, acknowledging achievements, and dealing promptly with lapses. A patient's motivation to change their way of life fluctuates according to mood and circumstance, and patient and doctor can feel deflated by early setbacks (see Chapter 11).

The primary care team is ideally suited to provide long term support. Barriers to change (see Chapter 12) need to be identified: some patients will have few barriers; others will have serious impediments that need to be addressed.

Dependence—detoxification

Some patients will find it hard to cut down or stop drinking because they experience **withdrawal symptoms**. At first, these may not be recognised for what they are and may be described as feeling nervous without a drink or not being able to function effectively until the first drink of the day. Other features in patients who are physically dependent will provide supportive evidence. They vary in severity: when mild they can be dealt with by rest, relaxation, and reassurance. An explanation that withdrawal symptoms are evidence that the brain has adapted to living in an alcoholic environment and will take time to adjust to one that is alcohol free is helpful. For a patient to know that symptoms, however unpleasant, will pass in a few days is very reassuring. This approach is often enough when patients are alcohol free at interview and report drinking <15 units a day in men and <10 units a day in women without recent withdrawal symptoms or recent drinking to relieve alcohol withdrawal.

When dependence is more advanced, the discomfort of withdrawal may necessitate medical detoxification. In most cases, this can be done at home, but in patients whose symptoms are very severe and other physical, psychological, and social factors are prominent, referral for specialist treatment in hospital will be necessary.

Benzodiazepines are the drug of choice in the management of withdrawal symptoms. Remember that they can induce temporary difficulties in cognition and recall. They are addictive if taken over time, **and detoxification with benzodiazepines should not be continued for more than seven days**. It is sensible to start with a high daily dose, such as 120 mg chlordiazepoxide or 40 mg diazepam on the first day, and then reduce the dose. After the third day, the dose should have been reduced by at least 25%. Details of the drug regimen should be adjusted to the patient's condition.

Drug treatment is only one part of the treatment for withdrawal. Patients and families should receive a careful explanation of the process, reinforced by an explanatory leaflet.

The most important therapeutic task when overcoming problems with alcohol is to engage the patient and retain them in treatment

---

Motivational interviewing

"People believe what they hear themselves say"

Empathic interviewing style
- Open ended questions
- Reflective listening
- "Get on their wavelength"

Feedback about risk
- Agree factual information about personal harm or impairment
- Balance sheet of pros and cons of changing/not changing

Roll with resistance
- Avoid confrontation
- Arguments about terms such as "alcoholic" are usually fruitless, particularly in the early stages

Support self efficacy
- Patient takes responsibility for achieving goals
- Choosing from menu of options
- Encourage belief that change is possible

Reinforce "self motivating statements"
- Recognition of harm caused
- Desire to change
- Feasibility of change

Alcohol withdrawal syndrome

Common features on stopping or reducing alcohol:
- Anxiety and agitation
- Tachycardia
- Sweating
- Tremor of extended hands, tongue, and eyelids
- Nausea and vomiting
- Insomnia
- Withdrawal fits
- Confusion
- Hallucinations

Withdrawal symptoms—indication for specialist/hospital referral

- Confusion
- Hallucinations
- Epilepsy or history of fits
- Risk of suicide
- Failed home detoxification
- Unsupportive home environment
- Acute physical or psychiatric illness
- Poor nutrition
- Any symptoms of Wernicke's encephalopathy

The patient should be advised to stay off work, not drive, rest, and drink plenty of fluids (fruit juice rather than stimulants such as coffee). The need to abstain from all alcohol should be made clear. Ideally, a community nurse or general practitioner should visit daily to monitor progress, review drugs, assess mental state, and vital signs, and, if possible, breathalyse for alcohol. Withdrawal symptoms usually resolve in 4-6 days, after which time the patient feels much better and optimistic about the future. They may believe they can now handle alcohol: that on no account should drinking (however little) be resumed should be made clear to patient and carers. The health professional who attends during this period is well placed to establish a therapeutic alliance for the future and reinforce the need for continued abstinence.

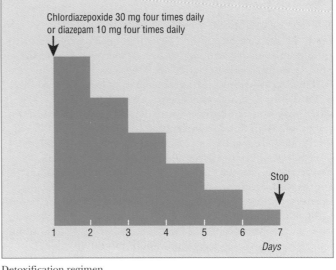

Detoxification regimen

Detoxification—daily check

- Tremor
- Pulse
- Temperature
- Blood pressure
- Level of consciousness
- Orientation
- Dehydration
- Evidence of continued drinking

Vitamins

No clear evidence shows that oral vitamins are needed for well nourished people with moderate alcohol dependence. In patients who are undernourished and have a history of frequent relapse and self-neglect, however, 200-300 mg thiamine a day over three months or longer is helpful to minimise the risk of damage to the brain and peripheral nervous system. Oral vitamins are absorbed poorly during the early stages of detoxification, so parenteral thiamine may be needed. If there is any doubt that the patient may have or be developing Wernicke's encephalopathy, urgent treatment in hospital with parenteral thiamine is needed (see Chapter 9 for details).

Other drugs are rarely necessary. Gaviscon will help relieve stomach pains. Anticonvulsants are of little value in preventing withdrawal fits, and the management of alcohol dependent people with established epilepsy is best supervised by a specialist clinic. Antidepressants are not indicated at this stage in treatment, and antipsychotics are needed rarely.

> **Many problem drinkers risk becoming dependent on benzodiazepines, which have been initiated over a series of failed detoxification episodes**

Wernicke's encephalopathy

Signs may include:
- Confusion
- Ataxia, especially truncal ataxia
- Ophthalmoplegia
- Nystagmus
- Comatose
- Hypotension
- Hypothermia
- Unexplained neurological signs during withdrawal

Requires urgent specialist assessment and treatment with parenteral thiamine

Relapse prevention

The drinker will need to devise strategies to cope with life without recourse to alcohol or with controlled drinking. Some will find it relatively easy to change this habit; this is often most true of those who identified the problem early and have not developed severe physical, social, and psychological problems.

The diary and balance sheet used in the initial assessment are useful tools throughout follow up, and they can be used to set goals and monitor progress.

Patients are encouraged to set their own goals and identify ways of dealing with triggers to relapse. If possible, involve the family in the plan and encourage persistence, even in the face of relapses. Sometimes major barriers to change that are not responding to motivational approaches will be obvious, and more specialist help will be required.

Triggers to relapse

Environment	• Availability
	• Pub atmosphere
Custom	• "Always" drink at certain times, occasions, and situations
Interpersonal	• Stress
	• Conflicts
	• Expectations
Intrapsychic	• Anxiety
	• Social phobias
	• Depression or elation (celebration)
Overconfidence	• Feeling good
	"I have got over my drinking problem"
	"I can take some alcohol again"

Pharmacotherapy

Disulfiram (Antabuse)

Disulfiram is a well established drug that acts as a deterrent to drinking by blocking the metabolism of alcohol to flood the system with the toxic substance acetaldehyde. This produces the disulfiram-alcohol reaction: flushing, palpitations, nausea, faintness, and in some cases collapse. Very rarely the consequences are serious or even fatal. Problems most often occur when high dosages are taken. An initial dose of 200 mg a day, if tolerated, can be increased after a few days to 400 mg; eventually a supervised dose of 400 mg two or three times a week is usually enough. Disulfiram should not be given in patients with significant active liver disease or cardiovascular disorders, in those who are pregnant, or are suicidal, or cognitively impaired. The action should be explained carefully to the patient and his or her family. Explanatory leaflets and a card explaining the actions of the drug should be carried.

The efficacy of disulfiram has been shown only when its usage is supervised, for instance by relatives or by clinic, primary care workers, or occupational health staff. Disulfiram interferes with the metabolism of other drugs, most notably tricyclic antidepressants, monoamine oxidase inhibitors, heparin, and some anticonvulsants. Drowsiness is noted by some users. Hepatotoxicity is a recognised risk and regular monitoring of liver function tests in the early months of treatment is advisable.

Acamprosate

Acamprosate (Campral) has proved helpful as an adjunct to psychological therapies. It should be started as soon as abstinence is achieved and can be continued during a relapse. If the patient makes good progress, it can be continued for one year. Dosage is 666 mg three times daily for patients aged 18-65 years who weigh >60 kg. Patients who weigh <60 kg should take 666 mg at breakfast, 333 mg at midday, and 333 mg at night. Side effects are rare and are mostly mild gastric upsets.

Naltrexone is a comparable drug, in that it also improves outcome and reduces the severity of relapse, but it is not yet licensed for regular use in the United Kingdom.

Referral

Referral to another agency should be timed carefully. Referral should not be too early because the patient may feel rejected; neither should it be too late, when the patient and family have become despondent or further damage has occurred. At the time of referral, a further follow up appointment should be made to find out whether they attended and how they got on. The dropout rate at the point of referral is high.

> Drug treatments should always be accompanied by psychological support and therapy aimed at attaining a longer term change of lifestyle that is essentially drug free

Further reading

- Edwards G, Marshall EJ, Cook CCH. *The treatment of drinking problems.* Cambridge: Cambridge University Press, 2003
- Freemantle N, Paramjit G, Godfrey C, Long A, Richards C, Sheldon T, et al. Brief interventions and alcohol use: are brief interventions effective in reducing harm associated with alcohol consumption? *Effective Health Care* 1993;7:1-13
- Fuller RK, Gordis E. Does disulfiram have a role in alcoholism treatment today? *Addiction* 2004;99:21-4
- Garbutt J, West S, Carey T, Lohr E, Crews F. Pharmacological treatment of alcohol dependence: a review of the evidence. *JAMA* 1999;281:1318-25
- Miller W, Wilbourne P. Mesa Grande: a methodological analysis of treatments for alcohol use disorders. *Addiction* 2002;97:265-77
- Slattery J, Chick J, Cochrane M, Craig J, Godfrey C, Kohli H, et al. *Prevention of relapse in alcohol dependence.* NHS Scotland: Health Technology Board for Scotland, 2002

Referral

- Make sure the patient knows why he or she is being referred and give a follow up appointment to review progress
- It is good practice to get to know the specialist resources available in your area as they vary considerably around the country

14   Resources

Bruce Ritson

For many people with alcohol related problems, the measures described in the previous chapters will be enough to help them cut down or stop drinking. For those who do not respond, are more severely addicted, or have other problems, specialist intervention or residential treatments may be needed.

Shared care

Specialist nurses attached to alcohol problems services are particularly well placed to collaborate with primary care teams, accident and emergency departments, and general medical and surgical wards to provide a combination of psychological therapy and supervised drug treatment. They also act as a bridge to other relevant agencies when necessary, sharing in the care of patients but leaving longer term support to the primary healthcare team.

The psychological behavioural treatments described below need some specialist training, which can be acquired by identified members of the primary healthcare team. Otherwise, the team members can work closely with a specialist nurse, counsellor, or psychologist.

Good evidence shows that clients who have a supportive network of family and friends have a better prognosis. **Social behavioural and network therapy** is a specific treatment that helps clients identify and use their network of supportive friends and family, who are then recruited to support the therapeutic task and not collude with relapse and evasions. Results from a controlled trial of this approach in the United Kingdom are awaited.

No single approach suits all patients, and many specialist treatments combine elements of these with relapse prevention and more general supportive counselling methods. This lack of specificity and the diversity of problems experienced by problem drinkers combine to make evaluation of treatments very complex.

Specialist services

The availability and character of specialist services varies considerably around the United Kingdom and the most important advice to any primary health care trust is to get to know local services, meet with them, and participate in the planning of alcohol services, thus influencing the decisions of local alcohol action teams and local training programmes.

Alcohol services within the NHS ideally should employ specialist nurses, psychologists, occupational therapists, and addiction specialist psychiatrists, but these are often in short supply and are overstretched. Some services will employ or have close links with counsellors, social workers, and probation workers. Many of these specialist teams will also deal with other forms of drug misuse and addiction. Some have an inpatient facility for detoxification, further assessment and treatment, but this is less common than formerly. Many services now rely on access to general or psychiatric wards when essential and referral to non-statutory residential care if indicated.

Alcohol counselling services

Many people with alcohol problems seek help from or are referred to counsellors who are part of Councils on Alcohol or

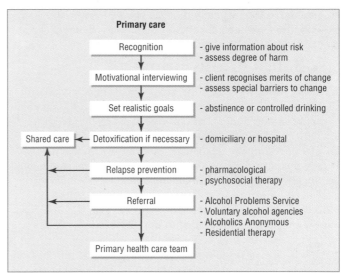

Example of care pathway

Psychological behavioural treatments of demonstrable effectiveness

- Coping skills training
- Behavioural self-control therapy
- Motivational enhancement therapy
- Marital relationship therapy

Specialist services

- Designate member of primary healthcare team to get to know local services on an individual basis?
- Identify Alcoholics Anonymous, Al-Anon member who will help with clients
- Know the philosophy and approaches followed by local alcohol agencies: residential facilities, etc
- Participate in local alcohol action team and highlight gaps in services

---

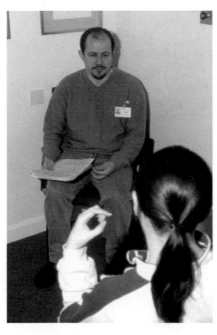

Alcohol services in the NHS employ specialists although they are often in short supply

voluntary agencies, supported by grants from health and local authorities. They may have links with occupational health services, prisons, and outreach services for the homeless and roofless. Alcohol in Employment Programmes promote early recognition and therapy for employees. They are very helpful in motivating clients whose job is secure, as long as they cooperate with treatment. Doctors and other healthcare workers should also know where to seek help for themselves and for their colleagues.

Alcoholics Anonymous

Alcoholics Anonymous is the best known and most successful self-help organisation in the world. Referral should be made in a considered way, and it is often best to arrange a specific contact with a known member who will take the client to their first meeting. Remember that Alcoholics Anonymous strongly believes that abstinence is the only solution for the alcoholic and this should be understood before referral. Members gain enormous support from each other and membership can continue over many years. Meetings are held throughout the country and most of the world, so that the benefits can be retained when travelling or moving to another area.

Al-Anon is a parallel organisation for partners, relatives, and friends, and it offers an opportunity for mutual support and understanding: membership does not require the drinker to attend Alcoholics Anonymous or even acknowledge that they have an alcohol problem. Al-Anon is especially valuable when heavy drinking has disrupted family life, with loss of self-esteem, money worries, and concerns about child care and disposal of property. Alateen is a somewhat similar organisation for the teenage children of alcohol misusers, who often experience unique difficulties as they grow up.

Group therapy

Alcoholics Anonymous has shown amply the value of fellowship and group processes in relapse prevention and sustaining recovery. Many formal therapies for alcohol problems also use groups as outpatients or as part of a residential programme. Groups can be based on cognitive behavioural or skill acquisition approaches or can use a more psychodynamic perspective. Some groups are predominantly supportive and open in their membership, while others are much more focused in their therapeutic task and more selective in their membership. Not all clients like the group process, but those who become involved usually value the experience.

Residential treatments

Although most clients respond effectively to outpatient or community based therapies, a minority may need longer term residential treatment.

Residential care
A number of residential programmes based on the Minnesota model use the tenets of Alcoholics Anonymous in group and individual therapy. Care often extends over months, with long term reunions and subsequent follow up through Alcoholics Anonymous. Residential homes also are provided by voluntary bodies, local authorities, and the probation service, which provide a "dry" house and rehabilitation programme for those who have lost all social support and are homeless or re-entering the community after periods in hospital or after imprisonment. The requirement of being dry or abstinent is not always attainable at first for some homeless, alcohol dependent people,

The telephone number of Alcoholics Anonymous can be found in the phone book and many branches have a 24-hour answering service

Alcoholics Anonymous Helpline 0845 769 7555

Alcoholics Anonymous groups differ in character, for instance, location, size, sex mix, and smoking policy

It is sometimes necessary to shop around before finding one that suits the needs of a particular client

Alateen has a range of publications aimed at the children of alcohol misusers. Photograph courtesy of Alateen

Benefits of group process
- Support from like minded people
- Identification with others with similar problems, reducing guilt and stigma
- Confront denial—defences recognised by other group members
- Explore new ways of dealing with old problems
- Quickly recognise relapse
- Mutual learning of new strategies
- Encourage lifestyle change

Indications for residential treatment
- Lack of social support
- Frequent relapses
- Difficulty grasping the need for abstinence
- Evidence of cognitive impairment

and many city centres have established "wet houses" where they can take the first steps towards more secure recovery.

Alcohol and crime

Alcohol is a very common factor in many crimes. Some voluntary agencies have established group programmes to re-educate problem drinkers, often using a cognitive therapy and skills based approach to minimise their risk of repeating the same mistakes. Throughout the country, similar programmes are organised for recidivist drink drivers (high risk offenders); these have been shown to reduce the likelihood of them repeating the offence.

Special needs

Some people need more specialist services because of the complex nature of their problem or because they are from a population that has difficulty accessing established services.

Dual diagnosis

Psychiatric disorders are common among people with alcohol problems. Some are directly related to the drinking and resolve when this is addressed. For some, however, a coexisting disorder also needs treatment, for instance, neurotic disorders and phobias where alcohol may have been used as a means of self-treatment to cope with the problem. People with serious and enduring mental illnesses, such as severe depression or schizophrenia, often have alcohol problems, and they find it hard to obtain help because they fall between the provision of mental health and addiction specialists. They have a poor prognosis, with frequent relapses and difficulty attending regular appointments. Specialist dual diagnosis teams are being established to combine the resources and skills of mental health and alcohol services—this approach considerably reduces the likelihood of relapse in both conditions. Dual dependencies also are increasingly common and again patients need the services of specialist substance misuse teams.

Cognitive impairment

Unfortunately, some people will have developed a degree of brain damage as a consequence of their drinking. For many, this will improve rapidly after a period of abstinence, and it is unwise to make any judgements about the long term extent of impairment until adequate vitamin therapy and improved physical health has occurred after at least three months of abstinence. Gloomy prognostications about the potential for recovery in Korsakoff's psychosis often are misplaced. Some people gradually will regain many of their former abilities or be able to adapt to their disabilities with appropriate psychological training. Nonetheless, some will need long periods of residential care; even then, training programmes and continued rehabilitation should not be abandoned, and progress should be reviewed regularly.

Groups who require special provision

Young people with binge patterns of drinking are a particular concern and often do not use primary healthcare team services. Opportunistic intervention—for instance in accident and emergency departments, the workplace, and youth work agencies—should give opportunities for brief interventions and recruitment into mainstream services if necessary. Similarly, people from **ethnic minority groups** may not feel able to use established services for a variety of reasons, and outreach workers need to attract appropriate care for this group—some of whom may feel severely stigmatised. **Older problem**

> Rehabilitation programmes in prison, and particularly on re-entry into the community, are a crucial part of preventing recidivism

---

Conditions directly related to alcohol, which resolve after drinking stops
- Delirium tremens
- Alcoholic hallucinations
- Most cases of depression resolve after a period of abstinence

---

Korsakoff syndrome
- Often, but not always preceded by Wernicke's encephalopathy
- Defect of recent memory, with relatively intact remote memory and intellect but a more mixed range of cognitive deficits, are very common
- Careful neuropsychological assessment is essential

Services such as Ethnic Alcohol Counselling in Hounslow work with individuals, family members, and carers primarily from minority ethnic communities who are affected by alcohol, drug, and mental health problems in order to help them make positive changes in their lives. Photogram courtesy of EACH

drinkers also feel the same; evidence also shows that the problem often is overlooked or disregarded by health professionals. This is unfortunate, because older drinkers often have an excellent response to treatment once the reason for drinking is identified and appropriate social support and help is given.

Homeless and roofless rough sleepers with alcohol problems present particular challenges, because it is hard to initiate change in an environment with little encouragement for an abstinent way of life. Outreach services have been developed to access rough sleepers and recruit them into appropriate hostels and then into their own tenancies. Continued support throughout this process is essential, including help with acquiring and sustaining basic skills in daily living. Many relapses occur at transitions between different services and locations, and the support of an identified carer throughout this recovery process is particularly important.

Women with alcohol problems often find it harder to access existing services, and their specific needs must be recognised. Once the drinking problem is acknowledged, the prognosis is generally good.

Self-help

Many people with alcohol related problems will themselves recognise that they need to cut down and stop drinking, and self-help can be very effective on its own or as an adjunct to brief intervention. Several useful self-help leaflets, helplines, and websites can be of assistance in changing habits.

Women with alcohol problems

Services need to be responsive to special needs such as:
- Accessibility—time and location
- Childcare concerns—childcare facilities and anxieties about child protection requirements
- Awareness of stigma—still prominent, particularly for the older woman
- Predominantly male client groups may deter; some women prefer single sex groups
- Past history of abusive relationships is common and needs appropriate therapy

Further reading
- Academy of Medical Royal Colleges Working Group. *The misuse of alcohol and other drugs by doctors.* London: British Medical Association, 1998
- Copello A, Orford J, Hodgson R, Tober G, Barrett C. Social behavior and network therapy. Basic principles and early experiences. *Addictive Behaviors* 2002;27:345-66
- Health Advisory Service. *Children and young people: substance misuse services—the substance of young needs.* London: Stationery Office, 2001
- Smith I, Hillman A. Management of alcohol Korsakoff syndrome. *Adv Psychiat Treat* 1999;5:271-8

Useful resources

Organisations
- The Medical Council on Alcohol, 3 St Andrew's Place, Regent's Park, London NW1 4LB (tel: 020 7487 4445; fax: 020 7935 4479; email: mca@medicouncilalcol.demon.co.uk; www.medicouncilalcol.demon.co.uk)
- Alcohol Concern, Waterbridge House, 32–36 Loman Street, London SE1 0EE (tel: 020 7928 7377; fax 020 7928 4644; email: contact@alcoholconcern.org.uk; www.alcoholconcern.org.uk)
- Alcohol Focus Scotland, 2nd Floor, 166 Buchanan Street, Glasgow G1 2LW (tel: 0141 572 6700; fax 0141 333 1606; www.alcohol-focus-scotland.org.uk)
- Institute of Alcohol Studies, 12 Caxton Street, London SW1H 0QS (tel: 020 7222 4001)
- Alcohol Education and Research Council, Room 520, Clive House, Petty France, London SW1H 9HD (tel: 020 7271 8379)

Self-help
- Alcoholics Anonymous (national helpline: 0845 769 7555; www.aa-uk.org.uk)
- Al-Anon family groups, 61 Great Dover Street, London SE1 6YF (tel: 020 7403 0888)
- Al-Anon, Mansfield Park, Unit 6, 22 Mansfield Street, Glasgow G11 5QP (24 hour telephone 0141 339 8884)
- Down your drink—online program for reducing drinking

Leaflets
- *Say when. How much is too much.* Alcohol Concern, 2004
- *Survival guide to drinking.* Health Education Board for Scotland, 2000
- *Alcofacts: a sensible guide to drinking.* Health Education Board for Scotland, 2003
- *So you want to cut down your drinking.* Health Education Board for Scotland, 2001

Book
- Goodwin D. *Alcoholism, the facts.* Oxford: Oxford University Press, 2000

Websites
- Health Education Board for Scotland, Woodburn House, Canaan Lane, Edinburgh EH10 4SG (www.hebs.scot.nhs.uk)
- Royal College of General Practitioners—training programme on alcohol (www.smmgp.co.uk)
- Greenfield S. *Alcohol on the brain: myths and mysteries.* www. aim-digest.com/gateway/pages/brain/articles/myths.htm

Index

Notes: As alcohol is the subject of this book, all index entries refer to alcohol unless otherwise indicated. Page references in *italics* refer to figures, tables or boxed material.

abrupt withdrawal effects 42
absorption rate variability 7, *7*
abstinence 41–2, 44
acamprosate (Campral) 48
accident and emergency departments 22–5
 attendance figures, alcohol-related 22
 collapse due to alcohol 24
 counselling 22, 23
 dependent drinkers 24–5
 detection *22*, 22–3
 education 23
 recognition of drinking problems 22
 referral 22, 23
 resuscitation 24
 role 22
 "top 10" conditions associated with alcohol 22, *22*
accident risk, blood alcohol level correlation 8–9
acetaldehyde 7, 48
acetate 7
acute toxic effects 2
adaptation difficulty 14
addicted drinkers *see* dependence (addicted drinker)
advertising, expenditure on *5*
advice and counselling 43–5
 abstinence 44
 accident and emergency department referral *22*, *23*, 23
 Alcoholics Anonymous 43
 balance sheet 43
 cutting down 44
 drinking diary 44, 45
 driving 44
 lifestyle changes 43–4
 motivation 43
 during pregnancy 44
 recommended daily intake 44
 relapses 43, 45, *45*
 review of goals 45
 sources *45*
 spouse involvement 44, *44*
age-related changes, disease protection 2
aggressive behaviour 4
alanine aminotransferase, misuse detection test 20
Al-Anon 41, 50
Alateen 41, 50
alcohol
 definition 10
 types *10*
Alcohol Concern and Medical Council on Alcohol *45*
alcohol consumption *see* consumption
alcohol content, of drinks
 calculation per drink *12*
 definition 10–11, *12*
 drinker types *11*
 standard drink 10
alcohol dehydrogenase 7
alcohol health worker 23, 24

Alcoholics Anonymous 24, 41, 43, 50
 contact details *45*
Alcohol in Employment Programmes 50
alcohol use disorders identification test (AUDIT) *18*, 18–19
alcohol withdrawal syndrome *see* withdrawal syndrome
alcolmeter 20–1
aldehyde dehydrogenase 7
 deficiency 13
 inhibition with disulfiram (Antabuse) 36
amphetamine (speed), alcohol interactions 37
analgesics, alcohol interaction 35, 37
Antabuse *see* disulfiram (Antabuse)
antisocial behaviour 4
anxiety reduction 44
arrestable offences after alcohol consumption 4, *4*
aspartate aminotransferase, misuse detection test 20
assault victim, surgical problems 30
atrial fibrillation ("holiday heart") 27
availability, drinking pattern association *14*
avascular necrosis of femoral head 32

balance sheet 43, *43*, 47
"basal narcosis" 33
behavioural effects 8
 alcohol levels affecting *8*
 individual differences 8
behavioural therapy *49*
benefits of alcohol consumption 2, 28–9, 34
benzodiazepines
 alcohol interaction 37
 withdrawal symptom treatment 46
binge drinking 4
 consumption pattern 1
 definition 11, *12*
 young adults 14
blood alcohol concentration 8
 accident risk 8–9
 behavioural effects 8
 correlation to breath/urine alcohol levels 20
 curve 8, *8*
 fatal concentrations 9
 legal driving limit 5, 20
 misuse detection 20
 rate of decrease in drinker types *9*
 risks associated *8*
 variation 7, 8
blood pressure 11
blood tests
 abnormal, medical problems 26
 detection of alcohol use 39, *39*
 see also specific tests
bone disorders, associated with heavy drinking *28*
bone healing 33
bottles, number of glasses by type of *10*
brain damage 27, 51

Index

breast cancer risk 11
breath alcohol level
    abstinence confirmation 45
    correlation to blood/urine level 20, *20*
    false positive results 20
    misuse detection 20–1
brief intervention 40, 46
burden of disease 2–3

caffeine, alcohol interaction 37
CAGE test 19, *19*
calories 7
Campral (acamprosate) 48
cancer 2, 31
    breast, risk 11
cannabis, alcohol interaction 38
carbimide 36
cardiomyopathy 27
cardiovascular problems 27, 34
care pathway *49*
causality, web *30*
cessation from drinking 41–2, 44
    conditions resolving after *51*
    see also detoxification
chest conditions, associated with heavy
        drinking *28*
child protection cases, alcohol involvement 5
children 5
    child protection cases 5
    drinking patterns 14
    resuscitation 24
    teenagers 5
chlordiazepoxide 46
chronic liver disease, mortality *2*
cirrhosis of the liver 27
    hepatitis C 38
    intraoperative problems 33
    morbidity 1–2, 27
    mortality 2, 28
    preoperative problems 31
    risks *1*
cocaine, alcohol interactions 37
cognitive behavioural therapy 44
cognitive impairment resources 51
cognitive therapy, crime (alcohol-related) 51
collapse due to alcohol 24, *24*
compartment syndrome 32, *32*
conditions associated with alcohol
    presenting in accident and emergency
        departments 22, *22*
    resolving after cessation *51*
    see also medical problems
constitution, mechanism underlying drinking 13
consumption, of alcohol 1–3, 14
    global *1*
    intake reduction 41–2, 44
    male vs female *15*
    recommended intake *see* recommended
        daily intake
    UK 1, *1*, 14
coronary heart disease protection 2, 28–9, 34
costs 2–3
    alcohol-related crime 5, 14, 22
    associated with misuse of alcohol 3, *3*
    drinks industry advertising expenditure *6*
    to industry 5, 14
    to NHS 3, 5, 22
    paramedic involvement 3
    primary care 3
Councils on Alcohol 49
counselling *see* advice and counselling

counselling services 49–50
cravings 24
crime and disorder 4–5
    costs 14, 22
    preventive/control measures 4–5
    resources 51
culture, affecting drinking *14*
Cushing's syndrome appearance 26, *26*
customs, affecting drinking *14*

definitions 10–12
delirium tremens (DTs) 24
demography, drinking patterns 14
dependence (addicted drinker)
    in accident and emergency departments 24, 24–5
    definition *11*, 12
    detoxification 42, 46–7, *47*
    features *12*
    management 41
    misuse statistics 15
    signs and management 24
detection of alcohol misuse *see* misuse, detection
detoxification 42, 46–7, *47*
    at home *42*
    medical 46
diazepam 46
distillation, definition 10
distribution of alcohol in the body 7, *7*
disulfiram (Antabuse) 48
    alcohol interactions 35, 36, *36*
    aldehyde dehydrogenase inhibition 36
divorce related to excessive drinking 5
domestic violence 41
dopamine (D2) receptor gene (A1 allele)
        presence 13
dopamine release 8
drink driving 4–5
    blood alcohol limit 5, 20
    casualties *5*
    resources 51
drinkers
    types, definitions *11*, 11–12
    typing by blood tests *39*
    see also specific groups
drinking
    mechanisms underlying *13*, 13–14, *14*
    types *11*, 11–12
drinking diary *44*, 45, 47
drinking patterns 13, 14–15
    influences affecting *13*, 13–14
drinks, number of glasses by type *10*
drinks industry advertising expenditure 6
driving
    advice 44
    behavioural effects 8–9
    see also drink driving
drug-alcohol interactions *35*, 35–8
    hepatitis C, liver cirrhosis 38
    illicit drugs 37–8
    legal drugs 35–7
    long-term alcohol use *37*
drug clearance, intraoperative problem 33
drunkenness, arrests for 4
dual diagnosis 42, 51
Dupuytren's contracture 32

ecstasy (MDMA), alcohol interactions 37
education, in accident and emergency
        departments 23
elderly *see* older people
elimination, of alcohol 7, 8

employment, workplace problems due to alcohol 5
environmental influences 13–14, *14*
enzyme induction in heavy drinkers 8
ethanol, definition 10
ethical attitudes to drinking 14
Ethnic Alcohol Counselling *51*
ethnic minorities 1, 51

facial appearances *26*
facial injuries *30*
false positive results
   breath alcohol levels 20
   urine alcohol levels 21
family history 13, 26
family support 41
fatal levels of blood alcohol concentration 9
femoral head, avascular necrosis of 32, *32*
fermentation, definition 10
fetal alcohol syndrome 27, 32, *32*
follow up 42
FRAMES 40, *40*

gamma hydroxybutyrate (GHB, liquid E, GBH),
   alcohol interaction 38
gastroenterology, preoperative problems 31
gastrointestinal bleeding, alcohol-related causes 31, *31*
gastrointestinal problems 27
   conditions associated with heavy drinking *28*
Gaviscon 47
gender differences in drinking patterns *15*
genetics, mechanism underlying drinking 13
Glasgow coma scale 24
global variation
   consumption 1
   standard drink 10
γ glutamyl transferase 39
   confirmation of abstinence 45
   misuse detection test 19, 20
goals, review of 45
gouty tophi *26*
government interest in alcohol 6
group therapy 50
   benefits *50*
gynaecological conditions, associated with
   heavy drinking *28*
gynaecomastia *26*

haemorrhagic stroke 1
haemostasis, postoperative problems 33–4
hangover effects 9
harmful drinking
   definition *11*, 12
   management of 41
   misuse statistics 15
hazardous drinking
   definition *11*, 12
   management of 41
   misuse statistics 15
head injury 24, 30
heart disease 2
   association with heavy drinking *28*
heavy drinking 8
   complications *27*
   conditions associated *28*
   definition 12
   legal drug reactions 37
   screening, questionnaires *17*
   suspicion of *27*
help groups 41, *45*, 52
   Al-Anon 41, 50
   Alateen 41, 50

Alcoholics Anonymous 24, 41, 43, *45*, 50
   key workers 41
hepatitis C 38
heroin, alcohol interaction 37
"holiday heart" (atrial fibrillation) 27
homeless people 5, 52
   residential treatments 50
hormonal changes, associated with heavy
   drinking *28*
hospital admissions 2, *2*
hospital referral, dependence 46
   see also referral
hyperkalaemia 32
hypertension 1, 27
hypnotics, alcohol interaction *35*, 35–6
hypoglycaemia 24–5

illicit drug-alcohol interactions 37–8
immune system problems
   associated with heavy drinking *28*
   postoperative 34
industry costs 14
intake recommendations *see* recommended
   daily intake
intake reduction 41–2, 44
   see also consumption, of alcohol
intoxication 8
intraoperative problems 30, 33, *33*
investigations in primary care 39–40

key workers 41, *41*
Korsakoff's psychosis *51*

laboratory tests
   confirmation of abstinence 45
   markers used *19*
   misuse detection 19–21, *20*
Licensing Act 2003 4
life events, drinking patterns *14*
lifestyle changes 43–4
liquid E (gamma hydroxybutyrate),
   alcohol interaction 38
liver
   cirrhosis *see* cirrhosis of the liver
   conditions associated with heavy drinking *28*
   enlargement 26

malignancy 2, 11, 31
MDMA (ecstasy), alcohol interactions 37
mean corpuscular volume 39
   confirmation of abstinence 45
   misuse detection test 19, 20
mechanisms underlying drinking *13*, 13–14
medical detoxification 46
medical problems 26–9, *27*
   abnormal blood test 26
   enlarged liver 26
   heavy drinking suspicion 27
   morbidity 27
   mortality 28
   problem drinker detection *see* problem drinking
   see also conditions associated with alcohol
men, alcohol intake *15*
menstrual disturbances 27
mental health problems, associated 2
metabolic changes 33
   associated with heavy drinking *28*
metabolic load in heavy drinkers 8
metabolism, of alcohol 7, 7–8
Michigan alcoholism screening test (MAST) 19
microsomal ethanol oxidising system 8, 33

Index

misuse (of alcohol)
  associated costs 3, *3*
  binge drinking 12
  definition 11–12
  detection *16*, 16–21, 22–3
    in accident and emergency departments 22, *22*, 23, *23*
    laboratory tests 19–21
    patient reluctance to discuss 16, *16*
    in primary care 39–40
    problem drinkers *26*, 26–7
    questionnaires 16–19, *17*, *18*, 22
    questions *16*, 16–19
    screening 23
  influences on risk *13*, 13–14
  management in primary care *see* primary care,
      alcohol misuse management
  mortality 1–2
  national enhanced service for 42, *42*
  patient acceptance 40, 41
  patient denial 40, 41
  social effects of 1, 30
  statistics 15
  warning signs in older patients 15
  see also specific types of drinkers
monoamine oxidase inhibitors, alcohol interaction 36
morbidity 1–2, 27
  postoperative *33*, 33–4
mortality 1–2, *2*, 28
  chronic liver disease *2*
motivation 22, 43
motivational interviewing 40, *40*, 46, *46*
muscle disorders, associated with heavy drinking *28*
myopathy 31–2
myths, about alcohol *10*

naive drinkers 11, *11*
naltrexone 48
national alcohol harm reduction strategy 6
National Drinkline *45*
nature of alcohol use 13–15
  drinking patterns 13, 14–15, *15*
  mechanisms underlying drinking *13*, 13–14
  misuse statistics 15
nervous system, associated with heavy drinking *28*
neuropathy 31
neuropraxia 31
neurosurgery, preoperative problems 31, 32
new general medical services contract 42
NHS
  alcohol services *49*
  costs (alcohol-related) 3, 22
nitrefazole 36
non-trauma surgical problems *see* surgical
      problems, non-trauma
nutrition inadequacy 27

obesity *26*, 27
obstetrics, preoperative problems 31, 32
occupation, drinking patterns *14*
older people 15, 51–2
  warning signs of misuse 15
opioids, alcohol interaction 37
orthopaedic surgery, preoperative problems 31–2
osteoporosis, preoperative problems 31
overdose (multiple substances) 24

Pabrinex 24, 25
Paddington Alcohol Test 16–17, *17*, 22, *23*
pancreatitis 31
paramedic involvement with alcohol 3
Parentrovite 24
patient acceptance 40, 41

patient confidence 16
patient denial 40, 41
peer pressure 43–4
persistent offenders, behavioural reform courses 4
pharmacotherapy 48
phenelzine, alcohol interaction 36
physical indications of alcohol misuse 39
physiological effects 7–9
politics
  of alcohol 5–6
  see also costs
poppers, alcohol interactions 38, *38*
postoperative problems 31, 33–4
  reasons for increased risk *33*
pregnancy
  advice and counselling 44
  alcohol consumption during 7
  morbidity during 27
  preoperative problems 31, 32
preoperative problems 30, 31–2
price, drinking pattern influence *14*
primary care, alcohol misuse management 39–42
  abrupt withdrawal effects 42
  abstention 41–2
  action plans *41*
  assessment of evidence 40, *40*
  brief intervention 40
  costs 3
  cutting down 41–2
  detection 39–40
  detoxification 42
  dual diagnosis 42
  families 41
  follow up 42
  group help 41
  motivational interviewing 40, *40*
  new general medical services contract 42
  patient acceptance 40, 41
  patient denial 40
  relapses 42
  shared care 40–1, *41*
problem drinking
  definition *11*
  detection 20, 26–7
  elderly 51–2
  misuse statistics 15
  see also misuse (of alcohol)
"protective effect" against disease 2, 28–9, 34
psychological indications of alcohol misuse 39

questionnaire use 39
  accident and emergency departments 22
  heavy drinking screening *17*
  misuse detection 16–19
questions, to discuss drinking habits 16, *16*

recognition of alcohol misuse, in A & E
      departments 22
recommended daily intake 11
  advice 44
redox state in heavy drinkers 8
referral 48
  from accident and emergency departments 22, 23
  in alcohol dependence 46
  of dependent drinkers 24, 46
relapses 42
  advice and counselling 43, 45, *45*
  prevention 47, 50
  triggers 45, *47*
religious attitudes to drinking *14*
reluctance to discuss drinking habits 16
renal conditions, associated with heavy drinking *28*

residential care 50–1
residential treatments 50–1
    indication *50*
resources 49–52
    Al-Anon 41, 50
    Alateen 41, 50
    alcohol and crime 51
    alcohol counselling services 49–50
    Alcoholics Anonymous *see* Alcoholics
        Anonymous
    group therapy 50
    residential treatments 50–1
    self-help 52
    shared care 49
    specialist services 49
    special needs 51–2
resuscitation 24
review of goals 45
rhabdomyolysis 32
risk associations, behavioural effects 8, 9
road traffic crashes, surgical problems 30
roofless rough sleepers 52

"Saturday night" palsy *31*
screening 23
sedatives, alcohol interaction *35*, 35–6
self-help resources 52
    see also help groups
self-reported consumption 39
sensible drinking definition *11*
serotonin release, behavioural effects 8
severity of alcohol dependence
        questionnaire 19
shared care 40–1
    pathway *49*
    resources 49
signs
    of alcohol misuse *39*
    of heavy drinking *27*
    of problem drinking *26*, 26–7
skid row drinker, definition 12
skin changes, associated with heavy drinking 28
social behavioural and network therapy 49
social consequences 1, 4, 30
social drinkers, definition *11*
social harm, definition 12
social indications of alcohol misuse 39
social situations, avoidance 43–4, *44*
social structure, drinking pattern influence *14*
specialist services 49
special needs resources 51–2
speed (amphetamine), alcohol interactions 37
spouse involvement in counselling 44, *44*
staff training in alcohol education 23
standard drink 10
street drinkers 5
stress response, postoperative problem 33
subdural haematoma *30*, 32

surgical problems 30–4
    non-trauma 30–4, *31*
        intraoperative 30, 33
        postoperative 31, 33–4
        preoperative 30, *31*, 31–2
    trauma 30

teenagers 5, 14
thiamine 47
tolerance 3
    heavy drinkers 8
    misuse detection with blood alcohol levels 20
tranylcypromine, alcohol interaction 36
trauma, surgical problems 30
treatment, alcohol misuse 46–8
triggers *43*
    avoidance/identification 44, 45, 47
    to relapse 45, *47*
triglyceride levels, misuse detection test 20
tyramine, alcohol interaction 36

United Kingdom
    consumption 1, *1*, 14
    standard drink 10
units of alcohol *10*
    safe, hazardous and harmful levels *11*
unsafe sex in teenagers 5
upper gastrointestinal bleeding 31, *31*
urate levels, misuse detection 19
urea, misuse detection 20
uric acid, misuse detection 20
urine alcohol levels 21
    correlation to blood/breath levels 19, *19*

ventricular arrhythmia 27
violent behaviour 4, 30
vitamin B, Wernicke's encephalopathy 24
vitamins 47

warfarin, alcohol interaction 35, 36
Wernicke's encephalopathy
    dependent drinkers 24, 25
    Pabrinex 24, 25
    signs *47*
    vitamin B 24
    vitamins 47
withdrawal symptoms *46*, 46–7
withdrawal syndrome 46, *46*
    postoperative problem 31, 34
women
    drinking patterns 14–15, *15*
    resources 52
    services for *52*
workplace problems due to alcohol 5
wound healing, postoperative problem 33

young adults (aged 16–24), drinking patterns 14
young people, resources 51